KU-417-745

ARABIC

Phrase Book & Dictionary

Nagi El-Bay

BBC Active, an imprint of Educational Publishers LLP, part of the Pearson Education Group, Edinburgh Gate, Harlow, Essex CM20 2JE, England

First published 2007.
Third impression 2010.

ISBN: 978-1-4066-1208-0

Cover design: Two Associates
Cover photograph: Andrew Catterall/Alamy
Insides design: Pentacor book design
Layout: Rana Salam Designs
Illustrations © Joanna Kerr, New Division
Development manager: Tara Dempsey
Series editor: Philippa Goodrich
Editor: Victoria El-Bay
Language consultant: Jonathan Featherstone
Senior production controller: Man Fai Lau

Printed and bound in China. CTPSC/03

The Publisher's policy is to use paper manufactured from sustainable forests.

how to use this book

This book is divided into colour-coded sections to help you find the language you need as quickly as possible. You can also refer to the **contents** on pages 4–5, and the contents lists at the start of each section.

Along with travel and language tips, each section contains:

 YOU MAY WANT TO SAY... language you'll need for every situation

 YOU MAY SEE... words and phrases you'll see on signs or in print

 YOU MAY HEAR... questions, instructions or information people may ask or give you

On page 14 you'll find **essentials**, a list of basic, all-purpose phrases to help you start communicating straight away.

Many of the phrases can be adapted by simply using another word from the dictionary. For instance, take the question fayn il maTar (Where is the airport?), if you want to know where the *station* is, just *substitute* il maHaTa (station) for il maTar to give fayn il maHaTa?

The **pronunciation guide** is based on English sounds, and is explained on page 6. If you want some guidance on how the Arabic language works, see **basic grammar** on page 169. The **English–Arabic dictionary** is on page 179.

We welcome any comments or suggestions about this book, but in the meantime, have a good trip – reHla Saᵃyeeda!

contents

pronunciation guide   **6**

the Arabic alphabet   10

the basics   **13**

essentials   14
numbers   16
ordinal numbers   18
fractions, days   18
months, seasons   19
dates, telling the time   20
time phrases   21
measurements   23
clothes and shoe sizes   25
national holidays and
  festivals   26

**general
conversation**   **27**

greetings   28
introductions   29
talking about yourself   30
asking about other
  people   32
chatting   33
the weather   34
likes and dislikes   35
feelings and opinions   36
making arrangements   38
useful expressions   39

travel&transport   **41**

arriving in the country   42
directions   43

information and tickets   46
trains   48
buses and coaches   50
underground   52
boats and ferries   54
air travel   55
taxis   57
hiring cars and bicycles   58
driving   60
mechanical problems   63
car parts   64
bicycle parts   66

accommodation   **67**

booking in advance   69
checking in   73
hotels, B&Bs and hostels   74
camping   77
requests and queries   78
problems and complaints   80
checking out   83
self-catering/
  second homes   84

food&drink   **87**

making bookings   89
at the restaurant   91
ordering your food   92
ordering your drinks   95
bars and cafés   97
comments and requests   99
special requirements   100
problems and complaints   102

paying the bill	102
buying food	103
menu reader:	
– general	106
– classic dishes	106
– ways of cooking	107
– meat	108
– fish	109
– general food	109
– desserts	114
– drinks	115

sightseeing &activities — 117

at the tourist office	118
opening times	119
visiting places	120
going on tours and trips	124
tourist glossary	125
entertainment	126
booking tickets	128
at the show	129
sports and activities	130
at the beach, river or pool	133

shops &services — 135

shopping	136
paying	139
buying clothes and shoes	140
changing rooms	141

exchanges and refunds	142
bargaining	143
photography	144
at the tobacconist	145
buying alcohol	146
at the post office	146
at the bank	148
changing money	149
telephones	150
mobiles	151
the internet	152
faxes	152

health&safety — 153

at the chemist's	154
at the doctor's	155
describing your symptoms	156
medical complaints and conditions	158
parts of the body	161
at the dentist's	163
emergencies	164
police	166
reporting crime	167

basic grammar — 169

English – Arabic dictionary — 179

pronunciation guide

Arabic pronunciation is quite regular, and only a couple of the Arabic sounds are difficult for English speakers. If you follow the guide, pronunciation shouldn't be a problem.

Most Arabic words are stressed. As a general rule this falls on the last but one syllable in a word. In this book, a stressed syllable is shown in bold type: e.g. *gowzi*. However, you need to be aware that the stressed syllable can change according to a word's ending or its position in the sentence - and it can vary from country to country, too!

✳ vowels

LETTER	SHOWN IN BOOK AS	APPROX ENGLISH EQUIVALENT	EXAMPLE	
أ	a	**a** as in 'h**a**t' (short) or	*gamal*	جمل
	aa	**a** as in 'c**a**r' (long) or	*Taar*	طار
	ae	**ae** as in 'a**e**roplane	*kitaeb*	كتاب
و	o	**o** as in 'd**o**ll' or	*foll*	فل
	ow	**ow** as in 'kn**ow**' or	*yowm*	يوم
	oo	**oo** as in 'b**oo**t'	*noor*	نور
ى	i	**i** as in 'h**i**t' or	*min*	من
	ee	**ee** as in 'k**ee**n'	*meen*	مين

* compound vowels

LETTER	SHOWN IN BOOK AS	APPROX ENGLISH EQUIVALENT	EXAMPLE	
أى	ai	**ai** as in '**ai**sle' or	*raiyiH*	رايح
	ay	**ay** as in '**day**'	*fayn*	فين
أو	ow	**ow** as in '**now**'	*gaw*	جو
	e	**e** as in '**e**gg'	*hena*	هنا
و	ew	**ay-oo**	*bitewga*ᵃ	بتوجع

* consonants

The capital letters *S, T, D* and *Z* are used in this book to represent 'heavy' or 'thick' versions of *s, t, d* and *z*. They're pronounced with the tip of the tongue touching the roof of the mouth against the front teeth. *H* represents another 'thick' letter, pronounced with the back of the tongue almost touching the back of the mouth, producing a 'strangled' *h* sound.

The sound *v* appears in some words borrowed from other language, e.g. 'video' (*vidyo*). It is written as ف.

Where the pronunciation shows double consonants, these must both be pronounced to give a long sound, e.g. *Salla* ('hall') is pronounced *Sal-la*.

If a word ends in a 'thick' consonant and the following word also begins with a consonant, a 'helping' vowel is placed between the two to avoid the difficulty of pronouncing them together, e.g. *noSSi keeloo* (half a kilo).

LETTER	APPROX. ENGLISH EQUIVALENT	SHOWN IN BOOK AS	EXAMPLE	
ء	glottal stop, as in cockney 'bu'er'	'	ma'aes	مقاس
ب	**b** as in '**b**ay'	b	baeb	باب
ت	**t** as in '**t**ea'	t	taeb	تاب
ث	**th** as in '**th**ink' or	th	thawra	ثورة
	s as in '**s**ee' or	s	sabit	ثابت
	t as in '**t**ea'	t	taªlab	ثعلب
ج	**g** as in '**g**ap' or	g	gamal	جمل
	j as in '**J**im'	j	jadeed	جديد
ح	thick **h**, as if you're breathing on glass before polishing	H	Haarb	حرب
خ	**ch** as in Scottish '**lo**ch'	kh	khabaT	خبط
د	**d** as in '**d**og'	d	dorg	درج
ذ	**z** as in '**z**oo' or	z	zahab	ذهب
	d as in '**d**og'	d	dahab	دهب
ر	**r** as in '**r**abbit', rolled like the Scottish '**r**'	r	ragil	رجل
ز	**z** as in '**z**oo'	z	zatoon	زيتون
س	**s** as in '**s**ign'	s	sabt	سبت
ش	**sh** as in '**sh**ore'	sh	shams	شمس
ص	'thick' **s**	S	maSaSa	مصاصة
ض	'thick' **d**	D	min faD lak	من فضلك
ط	'thick' **t**	T	baTee kha	بطيخة
ظ	'thick' **z**	Z	manZar	منظر

ع	almost silent, a sound between a glottal stop and French 'r' (like a very brief gargle)	^a	^a*arabi*	عربى
غ	a cross between Scottish 'ch' and French 'r'	gh	*ghaeli*	غالى
ف	**f** as in '**f**ood'	f	*fannaen*	فنان
ق	not found in English; similar to k but produced further back in the throat	q	*qahira*	قاهرة
ك	**k** as in '**k**ettle'	k	*kalb*	كلب
ل	**l** as in '**l**ike'	l	*lazeez*	لذيذ
م	**m** as in '**m**eat'	m	*midaen*	ميدان
ن	**n** as in '**n**ice'	n	*naedi*	نادى
ه	**h** as in '**h**ere'	h	*haram*	هرم
و	**w** as in '**w**indows'	w	*waedi*	وادى
ى	**y** as in '**y**es'	y	*yaman*	يمن

The article *(il or al)* loses its 'l' when followed by a word beginning with *t, d, r, z, a, s, sh, S, D, T, Z, l* or *n*, e.g. الدواء (*il dawa*, 'the medicine') may be pronounced *addawa*, and الرحلة (*il reHla*, 'the journey') becomes *irreHla*.

Some letters are pronounced differently in colloquial Egyptian from classical Arabic. For example, *th* is not used for the letter ث in colloquial Egyptian Arabic; instead, it is usually pronounced as *t* or *s*. The same is true of the letter ذ which is pronounced *z* in classical Arabic, but in colloquial Egyptian Arabic comes out as *d*.

✳ the Arabic alphabet

The Arabic alphabet has 28 characters. A character has different forms depending on whether it's used by itself or comes at the beginning, middle or end of a word.

ISOLATED	INITIAL	MIDDLE	FINAL	NAME	SHOWN AS
ا	ﺍ	ﺎ	ﺎ	*alif*	a, aa, ae
ب	ﺑ	ﺒ	ب	*ba'*	b
ت	ﺗ	ﺘ	ت	*ta*	t
ث	ﺛ	ﺜ	ﺚ	*thae*	th, t
ج	ﺟ	ﺠ	ﺞ	*geem or jeem*	g, j
ح	ﺣ	ﺤ	ﺢ	*Haa'*	H
خ	ﺧ	ﺨ	ﺦ	*khaa'*	kh
د	د	ﺪ	ﺪ	*dael*	d
ذ	ذ	ﺬ	ﺬ	*zael*	z,d
ر	ر	ﺮ	ﺮ	*re*	r
ز	ز	ﺰ	ﺰ	*zayn*	z,d
س	ﺳ	ﺴ	ﺲ	*seen*	s
ش	ﺷ	ﺸ	ﺶ	*sheen*	sh
ص	ﺻ	ﺼ	ﺺ	*SaaD*	S
ض	ﺿ	ﻀ	ﺾ	*DaaD*	D
ط	ط	ﻄ	ﻂ	*Ta*	T
ظ	ظ	ﻈ	ﻆ	*Zaa*	z,d
ع	ﻋ	ﻊ	ﻊ	*ªayn*	ª
غ	ﻏ	ﻐ	ﻎ	*ghayn*	gh
ف	ﻓ	ﻔ	ﻒ	*fa'*	f
ق	ﻗ	ﻘ	ﻖ	*qaaf*	q
ك	ﻛ	ﻜ	ﻚ	*kaf*	kh

pronunciation guide

ل	ـل	ـلـ	ل	*laem*	*l*
م	ـم	ـمـ	م	*meem*	*m*
ن	ـن	ـنـ	ن	*noon*	*n*
ه	ـه	ـهـ	ه	*ha'*	*h*
و	و	و	و	*waaw*	*w*
ي	ـي	ـيـ	ى	*ya'*	*y*

The letter ج *(geem)* is pronounced as a hard **g** (as in 'get') in Egypt, while in most other countries it is soft, more like an English **j**.

In the Arabic script there are also three vowel signs: ´ (*a*), ´ (*u*), and ˍ (*i*). These are written either above or below the letter to which they belong (although they are often left out), and they change the sound of that letter accordingly.

عَرب *arab* (Arab)   عَربي *arabi* (Arabic)
صبُون *Saboon* (soap)   بِنت *bint* (girl)

This is why you will notice that in this book sometimes only one written option is given in the Arabic for a word that has a masculine/feminine version in the imitated pronunciation.

Arabic text is written horizontally, from right to left. There are no capital letters. Punctuation is the same as in English, but written back to front, e.g. ؟ instead of ?.

✳ 'sun' and 'moon' letters

Of the 28 letters in the Arabic alphabet 14 letters are 'sun' letters, the other 14 are 'moon' letters. It is important to know which are which when using the definite article **il-**.

The letter *ba* is a 'moon' letter, so to define the word *bayt* add the definite article *il*:

il bayt   (the house)

When we define a word which begins with a 'sun' letter we do not pronounce the *l* in *il*, it is replaced with the first letter of the word in question. For example, to define (*il*) *saiyaara* replace the *l* with *s*:

issaiyaara   (the car)

In written Arabic there is no change in the spelling, you have to learn which letters are 'sun' letters.

SUN	شمسي	MOON	قمري
dael	د	*alif*	أ
zael	ذ	*ba'*	ب
zayn	ز	*jeem*	ج
Ta	ط	*Haa'*	ح
Zaa	ظ	*khaa'*	خ
noon	ن	*waaw*	و
SaaD	ص	*ya'*	ي
DaaD	ض	*meem*	م
seen	س	*kaf*	ك
sheen	ش	*qaaf*	ق
re	ر	*fa'*	ف
ta	ت	*ªayn*	ع
thae	ث	*ghayn*	غ
laem	ل	*ha'*	ه

the basics

essentials	14
numbers	16
ordinal numbers, fractions, days	18
months, seasons	19
dates, telling the time	20
time phrases	21
measurements	23
clothes and shoe sizes	25
national holidays and festivals	26

*essentials

Hello.	أهلاً و سهلاً.	*ahlan wa **sahlan***
Goodbye.	مع السلامة.	*ma^aassalaema*
Good morning.	صباح الخير.	*SabaH il **kheer***
Good evening.	مساء الخير.	*misa' il **kheer***
Good night.	تصبح على خير/تصبحى على خير.	*tisbaH ^aala kheer* (to m)/*tisbaHi ^aala kheer* (to f)
Yes.	أيوه.	*ay**wa***
No.	لا.	*la'a*
Please.	من فضلك.	*min **faDlak*** (to m)/ ***faD**lik (to f)
Thank you (very much).	شكراً (جزيلاً).	*shokran (gazeelan)*
I (don't) understand.	أنا (مش) فاهم/فاهمة.	*ana (mish) **fae**him* (m) / ***fah**ma* (f)
I don't speak Arabic.	ما باتكلمش عربي.	*ma batkalimsh ^aarabi*
I only speak a little bit of Arabic.	باتكلم عربي بسيط.	*batkalim ^aarabi baseeT*
Is there anyone who speaks English?	فى حد بيتكلم أنجليزى.	*fi Had biyetkalim ingleezi*
Pardon?	لامؤأخزة.	*la mo'**akh**za*
Could you repeat that please?	كمان مرة من فضلك.	*kaman **mar**ra min **faD**lak* (to m)/***faD**lik* (to f)
More slowly, please.	على مهلك.	*^aala **mah**lak* (to m)/ ***mah**lik* (to f)

the basics

14

How do you say it in Arabic?	كيف أقولها بالعربى؟	*kif a'oolha bil ªarabi*
What does this mean?	يعنى إيه؟	*yaªnni ay*
Can you translate?	ممكن تترجم؟	*momkin tetargim*
Excuse me.	عن إذنك.	*ªan iznak* (to m)/ *ªan iznik* (to f)
I'm sorry.	أسف/أسفة.	*aesif* (m)/*asfa* (f)
Cheers!	فى صحتك/صحتكم!	*fi SeHetak* (to m)/ *fi SeHetik* (to f)/ *fi SeHetkom* (to mixed group)
What's this?	إيه ده؟	*ay da*
Do you have...?	عندك...؟	*ªandak* (to m)/*ªandik* (to f)
How much is it?	بكام؟	*bikaem*
What time...?	الساعة كام...؟	*...issaªa kaem*
Where is/are...?	فين...؟	*fayn...*
Can you...	ممكن...؟	*momkin...*
Can you show me on the map?	ممكن تورينى على الخريطة؟	*momkin tewareenee ªala il khareeTa*
Can you write it down?	ممكن تكتبها؟	*momkin tiktibha*
Help!	ممكن تساعدنى؟/ ممكن تساعدينى؟	*momkin tisaªedni* (to m)/*momkin tisaªedini* (to f)

* numbers

0	٠	صفر	*Sefr*
1	١	واحد/واحدة	*waHid* (m), *waHda* (f)*
2	٢	أثنين	*itnayn*
3	٣	ثلاثة	*talaeta*
4	٤	اربعة	*arbaᵃa*
5	٥	خمسة	*khamsa*
6	٦	ستة	*setta*
7	٧	سبعة	*sabᵃa*
8	٨	ثمانية	*tamanya*
9	٩	تسعة	*tesᵃa*
10	١٠	عشرة	*ᵃashra*
11	١١	أحدى عشر	*Hidashar*
12	١٢	اثنى عشر	*itnashar*
13	١٣	ثلاثة عشر	*talatashar*
14	١٤	اربعة عشر	*arbaᵃtashar*
15	١٥	خمسة عشر	*khamastashar*
16	١٦	ستة عشر	*sitashar*
17	١٧	سبعة عشر	*sabaᵃtashar*
18	١٨	ثمانية عشر	*tamantashar*
19	١٩	تسعة عشر	*tesaᵃtashar*
20	٢٠	عشرين	*ᵃishreen*
21	٢١	واحد وعشرين	*waHid wi ᵃishreen*
22...	٢٢...	أثنين وعشرين	*itnayn wi ᵃishreen*
30	٣٠	ثلاثين	*talaeteen*
31	٣١	واحد و ثلاثين	*waHid wi talaeteen*
32...	٣٢...	أثنين و ثلاثين	*itnayn wi talaeteen*
40	٤٠	أربعين	*arbᵃeen*
50	٥٠	خمسين	*khamseen*

60	٦٠	ستين	*seteen*
70	٧٠	سبعين	*sabaeen*
80	٨٠	ثمانين	*tamaneen*
90	٩٠	تسعين	*tesaeen*
100	١٠٠	مائة	*maya*
101	١٠١	مائة و واحد	*maya wi waHid*
102...	١٠٢...	مائة و أثنين	*maya wi itnayn*
200	٢٠٠	مأتان	*mitayn*
250	٢٥٠	مأتان و خمسين	*mitayn wi khamseen*
300	٣٠٠	ثلثمائة	*toltomaya*
400	٤٠٠	ربعمائة	*robaomaya*
500	٥٠٠	خمسمائة	*khomsomaya*
600	٦٠٠	ستمائة	*sotomaya*
700	٧٠٠	سبعمائة	*sobaomaya*
800	٨٠٠	ثمانمائة	*tomnomaya*
900	٩٠٠	تسعمائة	*tosaomaya*
1,000	١,٠٠٠	الف	*alf*
2,000	٢,٠٠٠	الفين	*alfayn*
3,000	٣,٠٠٠	ثلاثة الاف	*talatalaef*
4,000	٤,٠٠٠	اربعة الاف	*arbaatalaef*
5,000	٥,٠٠٠	خمسة الاف	*khamastalaef*
100,000	١٠٠,٠٠٠	مائة الف	*meet alf*
one million	١٠٠٠,٠٠٠	مليون	*miliown*

Note: * The number one has two forms, for use with masculine (m) and feminine (f) nouns.

Arabic composite numerals are written from left to right, as in English, e.g. 1993 = ١٩٩٣ ; 25 piastres = ٢٥ قرش

* ordinal numbers

first	أولاً	*awwalan*
second	ثانياً	*taenayan*
third	ثالثاً	*taelithan*
fourth	رابعاً	*rabeªan*
fifth	خامساً	*khaemisan*
sixth	سادساً	*saedisan*
seventh	سابعاً	*saebeªan*
eighth	ثامناً	*taeminan*
ninth	تاسعاً	*taeseªan*
tenth	عاشراً	*ªaashiran*

* fractions

a quarter	ربع	*robª*
a half	نصف	*noS*
three-quarters	ثلاثة أربع	*talaet irbaª*
a third	ثلث	*tilt*
two-thirds	ثلثين	*tiltayn*

* days

Monday	يوم الأثنين	*yowm il itnayn*
Tuesday	يوم الثلاثاء	*yowm ittalaet*
Wednesday	يوم الأربعاء	*yowm il arbaª*
Thursday	يوم الخميس	*yowm il khamees*
Friday	يوم الجمعة	*yowm il gomªa*
Saturday	يوم السبت	*yowm issabt*
Sunday	يوم الأحد	*yowm il Had*

* months

January	يناير	*yanayer*
February	فبراير	*fabrayer*
March	مارس	*maeris*
April	أبريل	*ibreel*
May	مايو	*mayo*
June	يونيو	*yonyo*
July	يوليو	*yoolyo*
August	أغسطس	*aghosTos*
September	سبتمبر	*sebtambir*
October	أكتوبر	*oktobar*
November	نوفمبر	*novambir*
December	ديسمبر	*disambir*

* seasons

spring	الربيع	*irrabee*[a]
summer	الصيف	*iSSayf*
autumn	الخريف	*il khareef*
winter	الشتاء	*ishsheta*

the basics

19

dates, telling the time

✳ dates

YOU MAY WANT TO SAY...		
What day is it today?	النهارده أية؟	innaharda ay
What date is it today?	النهارده كام فى الشهر؟	innaharda kaem fishahr
When is your birthday?	عيد ميلادك أمتى؟	ªeed milaedak/ milaedik emta
(It's) the fifteenth of April.	خمسة عشر ابريل.	khamastashar ibreel
On the twenty-fifth of April.	يوم خمسة و عشرين ابريل.	yowm khamsa wi ªishreen ibreel

✳ telling the time

YOU MAY WANT TO SAY...		
What time is it?	الساعة كام؟	issaªa kaem
What time does it open?/close?	بيفتح /بيقفل الساعة كام؟	biyeftaH/biy'fil issaªa kaem
What time does it start?/finish?	بيبدأ/ بيخلص الساعة كام؟	biyebda'/biyekhlaS issaªa kaem
It's...	الساعة...	issaªa...
10 o'clock	عشرة	ªashra
midday	الظهر	iDDohr
midnight	نصف الليل	noS ilayl
At...	الساعة...	issaªa...
half past nine	تسعة و نصف	tesªa wi noS
half past ten	عشرة و نصف	ªashra wi noS

the basics

20

quarter past nine	تسعة و ربع	tes^aa wi rob^a
quarter to ten	عشرة الا ربع	^aashra ila rob^a
twenty past ten	عشرة وثلث	^aashra wi tilt
twenty-five to ten	تسعة ونصف وخمسة	tisaa wi nos wi khamsa
precisely ten o'clock	عشرة بالظبط	^aashra bil zabt
In...	كمان...	kamaen...
ten minutes	عشر دقائق	^aashar d'ayi'
fifteen minutes	ربع ساعة	rob^a sa^aa
half an hour	نصف ساعة	noS i sa^aa
an hour	ساعة	sa^aa

* time phrases

YOU MAY WANT TO SAY...

day	يوم	yowm
week	أسبوع	izboo^a
fortnight	أسبوعين	izboo^aayn
month	شهر	shahr
year	سنة	sana
today	النهاردة	innaharda
tomorrow	بكرة	bokra
the day after tomorrow	بعد بكرة	ba^ad bokra
yesterday	أمبارح	imbariH
the day before yesterday	أول أمبارح	awil imbariH

the basics

21

time phrases

this morning	النهار ده الصبح	*innaharda iSSobH*
this afternoon/ evening	النهار ده بعد الظهر	*innaharda ba°d iDDohr*
tonight	النهاردة بالليل	*inaharda bilayl*
on Friday	يوم الجمعة	*yawm il gom°a*
on Fridays	أيام الجمعة	*ayyaem il gom°a*
every... Friday week	كل... يوم جمعة أسبوع	*kol...* *yowm gom°a* *izboo°*
for... a week two weeks two years	لمدة... أسبوع أسبوعين سنتين	*limodit...* *izboo°* *izboo°ayn* *sanatayn*
I'm here for two weeks.	أنا هنا أسوعين.	*ana hena izboo°ayn*
I've been here for a month.	بقى لى شهر.	*ba'aeli shahr*
I've been learning Arabic for two years.	بأدرس عربى بقى لى شهرين.	*badris °arabi ba'aeli shahrayn*
next Tuesday	الثلاثاء اللى جاى	*ittalaet ili gaiy*
next week	الأسبوع اللى جاى	*il izboo° ili gaiy*
next month	الشهر اللى جاى	*ishshahr ili gaiy*
next year	السنة الجاية	*issana igaiya*
last night	امبارح بالليل	*imbariH bilayl*
last week	الأسبوع اللى فات	*il izboo° ili faet*
a week ago	من أسبوع	*min izboo°*
a year ago	من سنة	*min sana*

the basics

22

Since...	...من	*min*
yesterday	أمبارح	*imbariH*
last week	الأسبوع اللى فات	*il izbooᵃ ili faet*
last month	الشهر اللى فات	*ishshahr ili faet*
last year	السنة اللى فاتت	*issana ili faetit*
(in) the morning/ afternoon	الصبح/بعد الظهر	*iSSobH/baᵃd iDDohr*
in six months' time	بعد ست شهور	*baᵃd set shohoor*
(at) night	بالليل	*bilayl*
it's early	بدرى	*badri*
it's late	متأخر	*met'akhar*

✳ measurements

MEASUREMENTS

centimetres	سنتيمتر	*santimeeter*
metres	متر	*meeter*
kilometres	كيلومتر	*keelometr*
miles	أميال	*amiyael*
a litre	لتر	*litr*
25 litres	خمسة و عشرين لتر	*khamsa wi ᵃishreen litr*
gramme	جرام	*gram*
100 grammes	مائة جرام	*meet gram*
200 grammes	مأتان جرام	*mitayn gram*
kilo(s)	كيلو	*keeloo*

measurements

CONVERSIONS

10cm = *4 inches*	**1oz** = *28g*
50cm = *19.6 inches*	**100g** = *3.5oz*
1 metre = *39.37 inches*	**¼lb** = *113g*
110 metres = *100 yards*	**½lb** = *225g*
1km = *0.62 miles*	**1lb** = *450g*
1 mile = *1.61km*	**½ kilo** = *1.1lb*
1 inch = *2.45cm*	**1 kilo** = *2.2lb*
1 foot = *30cm*	**1 litre** = *1.8 pints*

To convert kilometres to miles, divide by 8 and multiply by 5 e.g. 16 kilometres (16 / 8 = 2, 2 x 5 = 10) = 10 miles.

For miles to kilometres, divide by 5 and multiply by 8 e.g. 50 miles (50 / 5 = 10, 10 x 8 = 80) = 80 kilometres.

the basics

24

* clothes and shoe sizes

WOMEN'S CLOTHES

UK	8	10	12	14	16	18	20
Arab Countries	36	38	40	42	44	46	48

MEN'S CLOTHES

UK	36	38	40	42	44	46	48
Arab Countries	46	48	50	52	54	56	58

MEN'S SHIRTS

UK	14	14½	15	15½	16	16½	17
Arab Countries	36	37	38	39	41	42	43

SHOES

UK	2	3	4	5	6	7	8
Arab Countries	35	36	37	38	39	40	42
UK	9	10	11	12			
Arab Countries	43	44	45	46			

✳ national holidays and festivals

● Christian and Islamic feasts are celebrated at different times each year according to the Muslim or Christian calendar.

● Other days mark political and military achievements, and each country has its own public days of celebration or holiday. It is advisable to check with the relevant tourist office before planning a visit, to ensure that you do not arrive at a time when everything is closed.

MUSLIM

شهر رمضان	*shahr ramaDaan*	Ramadan (31 days)
عيد الفطر	*ᵃeed il fiTr*	The Breakfast Feast (3 days)
عيد الأضحى	*ᵃeed il aDHa*	The Biram Feast (4 days)
المولد النبوى	*il moolid innabawi*	The Prophet's Birthday (1 day)

CHRISTIAN

الكريسماس	*il krismas*	Christmas
رأس السنة	*ras issana*	New Year
عيد ميلاد المسيح	*ᵃeed milaed il maseeH*	Coptic Christmas (7 January)
عيد القيامة	*ᵃeed il qiyama*	Easter

greetings	28
introductions	29
talking about yourself	30
asking about other people	32
chatting	33
the weather	34
likes and dislikes	35
feelings and opinions	36
making arrangements	38
useful expressions	39

general conversation

Reference to God (Allah in Arabic) is frequent in general conversation, including greetings such as *Alaykom issalaem wa rahmatoollaH wa barakatoo*, meaning 'God's mercy and his blessings be with you'. Also frequently heard in response to any query is *il Hamdoo lillaH*, meaning literally 'thanks be to God', but often used instead of a simple 'yes'. Another very common phrase is the expression *insha' allah* meaning 'God willing'.

YOU MAY WANT TO SAY...

● Hello.	أهلاً و سهلاً.	*ah*lan wa *sah*lan
● Good morning.	صباح الخير.	*SabaH il kheer*
● Good afternoon/ evening.	مساء الخير.	*misa' il kheer*
● Good night.	تصبح على خير.	*tiSbaH ªala kheer*
● Goodbye.	مع السلامة.	*maªassalaema*
● Bye.	سلام.	*salaem*
● See you later.	أشوفك/أشفكم قريب ان شاء ألله.	*ashoofak* (to m)/*ashoofik* (to f)/*ashofkom* (to group) *oraiyib insha'allah*
● How are you? *(formal)* *(informal)*	كيف الحال؟ إذيك؟	*kaef il Hal* *izzayak* (to m)/ *izzayik* (to f)/ *izzayokom* (to group)

general conversation

How are things?	إيه الأحوال؟	*ay il aHwael*
Fine, thanks.	الحمد لله شكراً.	*il Hamdoo lillah shokran*
And you?	و أنت؟	*wenta (to m)/wenti (to f)*

✳ introductions

YOU MAY WANT TO SAY...

My name is...	أسمى...	*ismi...*
This is... *(referring to a man)*	هذا...	*haeza...*
Mr Brown	السيد براون	*issayed brawn*
my husband	زوجى	*zowgi*
my son	أبنى	*ibni*
my fiancé	خطيبى	*khaTeebi*
my friend	صديقى	*Sadeeqi*
This is... *(referring to a woman)*	هذه...	*haezihi...*
Miss Brown	الأنسة براون	*il aenisa brawn*
Mrs Brown	السيدة براون	*issayeda brawn*
my wife	زوجتى	*zowgti*
my daughter	أبنتى	*binti*
my fiancée	خطيبتى	*khaTeebti*
my friend	صديقتى	*Sadeeqti*
Pleased to meet you.	سعيد/سعيدة بمقابلتك.	*saᵃeed (m)/saᵃeeda (f) bimow'ablitak (to m)/bimow'ablitik (to f)*

✷ talking about yourself

YOU MAY WANT TO SAY...

● I'm English.	أنا أنجليزي/أنجليزية.	*ana ingleezi* (m)/ *ingleezaya* (f)
● I'm Scottish.	أنا سكوتلاندي/سكوتلاندية.	*ana iskotlandi* (m)/ *iskotlandaya* (f)
● I'm Irish.	أنا أيرلندي/أيرلندية.	*ana irlaendi* (m)/ *irlandaya* (f)
● I'm Welsh.	أنا من ويلز.	*ana min wayl*z
● I come from...	أنا من...	*ana min...*
England	أنجلترا	*ingil***terra**
Ireland	أيرلندا	*ayr***lan***da*
Scotland	سكوتلاندا	*skot***lan***da*
Wales	ويلز	***wayl***z
● I/We live in...	أعيش/نعيش في...	*aªeesh/naªeesh fi...*
London	مدينة لندن	*madeenit landan*
Edinburgh	مدينة أدنبرة	*madeenit edinbra*
● I'm 25 years old.	عندي ٢٥ سنة.	ªandi kham**sa** wi ªishreen **sana**
● He's/she's five years old.	عنده/عندها خمس سنين.	ªando/ªandaha khamas sineen
● I'm a...	أنا...	*ana...*
nurse	ممرض/ممرضة	*momarriD* (m)/ *momarriDa* (f)
student	طالب/طالبة	*Taalib* (m)/*Taaliba* (f)
● I work in/for...	أنا بأشتغل في...	*ana bashtaghal fi...*
a bank	بنك	*bank*

talking about yourself

- I'm unemployed. — أنا ما باشتغلش. — *ana ma bashtaghalsh*

- I'm self-employed. — أنا بأشتغل لحسابى — *ana bashtaghal li Hisaebi*

- I'm... — أنا... — *ana...*
  - married — متزوج/متزوجة — *motazawig* (m)/ *motazawiga* (f)
  - divorced — مطلق/مطلقة — *moTalla'* (m)/ *moTalla'a* (f)
  - separated — منفصل/منفصلة — *monfaSil* (m)/ *monfaSila* (f)
  - single — عازب/عازبة — *ªaezib* (m)/*ªaezba* (f)
  - a widower/ widow — أرمل/أرملة — *armal* (m)/*armala* (f)

- I have... — عندى... — *ªandi...*
  - three children — ثلاثة أطفال — *talaet aTfaal*
  - one brother — أخ واحد — *akh waHid*
  - two sisters — أختين — *okhtayn*

- I don't have... — معنديش... — *maªandeesh...*
  - any children — أطفال — *aTfaal*
  - any brothers or sisters — أخوات — *akhwaet*

- I'm on holiday here. — أنا هنا فى أجازة. — *ana hena fi agaeza*

- I'm here on business. — أنا هنا فى مهمة عمل. — *ana hena fi mohimit ªamal*

general conversation

31

asking about other people

I'm here with my...	أنا هنا مع...	*ana hena maªa...*
family	عائلتى	*ªa'ilati*
colleague	زميلى	*zameeli*
My husband/son is...	زوجى/أبنى...	*zowgi/ibni...*
My wife/daughter is...	زوجتى/أبنتى...	*zowgti/binti...*
I speak very little Arabic.	باتكلم عربى بسيط قوى.	*batkallim ªarabi baseeT awi*

✳ asking about other people

Where do you come from?	أنت من أى بلد؟	*inta* (to m)/*inti* (to f) *min ay balad*
What's your name?	أسمك إيه؟	*ismak* (to m)/*ismik* (to f) *ay*
Do you have...	عندك...	*ªandak* (to m)/ *ªandik* (to f)...
any children?	أطفال؟	*aTfaal*
any brothers and sisters?	أخوات؟	*akhwaet*
a girlfriend?	صديقة؟	*Sadeeqa*
a boyfriend?	صديق؟	*Sadeeq*
Are you married?	أنت متزوج/انت متزوجة؟	*inta motazawig* (to m)/*inti motazawiga* (to f)

general conversation

32

How old are you?	عندك كام سنة؟	ªan**dak** (to m)/ ªan**dik** (to f) kaem sana
How old are they?	عندهم كام سنة؟	ªan**do**hom kaem sana
Is this your... husband/wife?	هل ده/دى... زوجك/زوجتك؟	hael da/di... zow**gik**/ zow**gae**tak
friend (m/f)?	صديقك/صديقتك؟	Sa**dee**qik/ Sa**deq**tak
Where are you (pl) staying?	ساكنين فين؟	sak**neen** fayn
What do you do?	بتشتغل/بتشتغلى إيه؟	bitish**tagh**al (to m) /bitish**tagh**ali ay (to f)

✳ chatting

Alexandria is very beautiful.	أسكندرية جميلة قوى.	iskinde**ra**ya ga**mee**la **awi**
I like Morocco (very much).	أنا باحب المغرب (قوى).	ana ba**Heb** il **maghrib** (**awi**)
It's the first time I've been to Doha.	دى أول مرة أزور فيها الدوحة.	di awil **marra** a**zoor** **fee**ha ido**Ha**
I come to Cairo often.	انا بازور القاهرة كتير.	ana ba**zoor** il **qahera** kiteer
Do you live here?	أنت عايش هنا؟	inta ªa**yish** (to m)/ inti ªa**isha** (to f) **hena**

Are you from here?	أنت من هنا؟	*inta* (to m)/ *inti* (to f) *min hena*
Have you ever been to...	هل زرت...	*hael zort...*
Edinburgh?	إدنبرة؟	*edinbra*
London?	لندن؟	*landan*
Tunis?	تونس	*toonis*

YOU MAY HEAR...

عجبتك اسوان؟	*ªagabitak aswan*	Do you like Aswan?
زرت البحرين قبل كده؟	*zort il baHrayn abli keda*	Have you been to Bahrain before?
الزيارة لحد أمتى؟	*izziyaara liHad emta*	When are you here until?
بتتكلم عربى كويس جدآ.	*bititkalim ªarabi kwayyis gedan*	Your Arabic is very good.

✳ the weather

YOU MAY WANT TO SAY...

What a beautiful day!	يوم جميل!	*yowm gameel*
What fantastic weather!	الجو جميل جدآ!	*iggaw gameel gedan*
It's (very)...	الدنيا... (قوى)	*iddonya ... (awi)*
hot	حر	*Har*
cold	برد	*bard*

- It's windy.   الريح جامدة.   *irreeH gamda*
- What's the forecast?   النشرة الجوية بتقول إيه؟   *innashra iggawaya bit'ool ay*
- It's raining.   بتمطر.   *bitmaTar*

* likes and dislikes

YOU MAY WANT TO SAY...

- I like...   ...باحب   *baHeb...*
  - football   كرة القدم   *korit il qadam*
  - strawberries   الفراولة   *il firawla*
- I love...   بأحب ... قوى   *baHeb ... awi*
  - the beach   الشاطىء   *ishaaTi'*
  - bananas   الموز   *il mowz*
- I don't like ...   ...مش باحب   *mish baHeb...*
  - the rain   المطر   *il maTar*
  - tomatoes   الطماطم   *iTTamaTim*
- I hate...   ...بأكره   *bakrah...*
  - swimming   السباحة   *issibaHa*
- Do you like...   ...بتحب   *bitHeb (to m)/ bitHebi (to f)...*
  - walking?   المشى   *il mashi*
  - dogs?   الكلاب   *ikkilaeb*
- I like it (m)/him.   باحبه.   *baHeboo*
- I like it (f)/her.   باحبها.   *baHebaha*
- I like them.   باحبهم.   *baHebohom*

feeling and opinions

- I don't like it (m)/ him. | أنا ما باحبوش. | *ana ma baHeboosh*
- I don't like it (f)/her. | أنا ما باحبهاش. | *ana ma baHebahaash*
- I don't like them. | أنا ما باحبهمش. | *ana ma baHebahomsh*

✳ feelings and opinions

YOU MAY WANT TO SAY...

Are you...	انت...	*inta* (to m)/ *inti* (to f)...
all right?	كويس/كويسة؟	*kwayyis* (to m)/ *kwayyissa* (to f)
happy?	مبسوط/مبسوطة؟	*mabsooT* (to m)/ *mabsooTa* (to f)
sad?	زعلان/زعلانة؟	*za*ᵃ*laen* (to m)/ *za*ᵃ*laena* (to f)
Are you (very)...	أنت ... (قوى)	*inta* (to m)/ *inti* (to f)... *(awi)*
cold?	بردان/بردانة قوى	*bardaen* (to m)/ *bardaena* (to f)
hot?	حران/حرانة	*Haraan* (to m)/ *Haraana* (to f)
I'm...	انا...	*ana...*
tired	تعبان/ تعبانة	*ta*ᵃ*baen* (m)/ *ta*ᵃ*baena* (f)
bored	زهقان/زهقانة	*zah'aen* (to m)/ *zah'aena* (f)

general conversation

I'm a bit annoyed.	انا متضايق/متضايقة شوية.	*ana mit**Day**i' (m)/ mit**Day**'a (f) sho**wai**ya*
What do you think of...?	اية رأيك فى...؟	*ay **ra**'yak (to m)/ **ra**'yik (to f) fi...*
I/We think it's...	رأى/ رأينا أنه/انها...	*ra'yi/ra'yena **in**no (of m)/**in**naha (of f)...*
great	هايل/هايلة	*ha**e**yil (m)/ ha**e**yla (f)*
funny	مضحك/مضحكة	*mo**DH**ik (m)/ mo**DH**ika (f)*
Did you like it?	عجبتك؟	*ᵃaga**bi**tak (to m)/ ᵃaga**bi**tik (to f)*
I/We thought it was...	اعتقد/نعتقد انه/أنها...	*aᵃ**ta**qid/naᵃ**ta**qid **in**no (of m)/**in**naha (of f)...*
beautiful	جميل/جميلة	*ga**meel** (m)/ ga**mee**la (f)*
awful	وحش/وحشة	*we**Hish** (m)/ we**H**sha (f)*
Do you like him/ it?	عاجبك؟	*ᵃa**ga**bak (to m)/ ᵃa**ga**bik (to f)*
Do you like her/it?	عاجبتك؟	*ᵃaga**be**tak (to m)/ ᵃaga**be**tik (to f)*
I like him/her.	عاجبني/عاجباني.	*ᵃa**geb**ni/ᵃag**bae**ni*
What's your favourite...	إيه ... المفضل؟	*ay ... il mo**fa**Dal*
film?	فيلمك	*fil**mak** (to m)/ fil**mik** (to f)*

● My favourite … is…	...المفضل هو...	...il mofaDal howa…
● How do people feel about…	إيه شعور الناس عن...	ay shoªoor innaes ªan
the government?	الحكومة؟	il Hokooma
the British?	الأنجليز؟	il ingeleez
drugs?	المخدرات؟	il mokhadarraat

* making arrangements

YOU MAY WANT TO SAY…

● What are you doing tonight?	حا تعمل/حاتعملى اية الليلة؟	Hateªmil (to m)/ Hateªmili (to f) ay illayla
● Would you like…	تحب/تحبى...	teHeb (to m)/ teHebi (to f)…
a drink?	مشروب؟	mashroob
something to eat?	تأكلى حاجة؟	takli Haega
to come with us?	تيجى معانا؟	teegi maªana
● Yes, please.	أيوة من فضلك.	aywa min faDlak (to m)/faDlik (to f)
● No, thank you.	لا شكرآ.	la shokran
● What time shall we meet?	نتقابل الساعة كام؟	nit'aebil issaªa kaem
● Where shall we meet?	نتقابل فين؟	nit'aebil fayn

See you...	...أشوفك	ashoofak (to m)/ ashoofik (to f)...
later	كمان شوية	kamaen showaiya
at seven	الساعة سبعة	issaªa sabªa
Sorry, we already have plans.	اسف/اسفة فى ترتيب سابق.	aesif (m)/asfa (f) fi terteeb saebiq
Please go away.	من فضلك ابعد/فضلك ابعدى/فضلكم ابعدوا عنا.	min faDlak ebªed (to m)/faDlik ebªedi (to f)/ faDlokom ebªedoo (to group) ªana
Leave us alone!	سيبنى فى حالى!	sebni fi Haeli
What's your email address?	عنوانك الألكترونى أيه؟	ªenwaenak il elektrowni ay
My email address is...	عنوانى الألكترونى هو...	ªenwaeni il elektrowni howa...

✳ useful expressions

(see **essentials**, page 14)

YOU MAY WANT TO SAY...

Congratulations!	مبروك!	mabrook
Happy Birthday!	عيد ميلاد سعيد	ªeed milaed saªeed
Happy Ramadan!	رمضان كريم	ramaDaan kareem
Happy Eid!	عيد مبارك	ªeed moobaarak

● Happy Christmas!	عيد سعيد	*ªeed saªeed*
● Happy New Year!	كل سنة وانت طيب! وانت طيبة! وانتم طيبين!	*kol sana wenta Tayyib* (to m)/ *wenti Tayyiba* (to f)/*wentom Tayyibeen* (to group)
● Good luck!	حظ سعيد!	*HaZ saªeed*
● That's... fantastic! terrible!	...ده هايل! يا ساتر!	*da...* *haeyil* *yasaetir*
● What a pity!	يا خسارة!	*yakhosara*
● Bless you!	ألة يكرمك!	*allah yikremak* (to m)/*yikremik* (to f)
● Have a good journey!	رحلة سعيدة	*reHla saªeeda*
● Enjoy your meal!	اكلة ممتعة	*akla momteªa*
● Thank you, same to you.	شكرآ وانت كمان.	*shokran wenta* (to m)/*wenti* (to f) *kamaen*
● Cheers!	فى صحتك/صحتكم!	*fi SeHetak* (to m)/*SeHetik* (to f)/*SeHetkom* (to group)

travel&transport

arriving in the country	42
directions	43
information and tickets	46
trains	48
buses and coaches	50
underground	52
boats and ferries	54
air travel	55
taxis	57
hiring cars and bicycles	58
driving	60
mechanical problems	63
car parts	64
bicycle parts	66

* arriving in the country

● EU citizens need a visa to visit most of the Arabic-speaking countries. It is advisable to check requirements before travelling.

YOU MAY SEE...

أستلام الحقائب	*istilaem il Haqa'ib*	baggage reclaim
بضاعة خارج المسموح بة	*booDaªa khaerig il masmooH boh*	goods to declare
تواليت	*twalit*	toilets
رجال	*rigael*	gents
سيدات	*sayedaet*	ladies
جمرك	*gomrok*	customs
خروج	*khoroog*	exit
مراقبة الجوازات	*moraqabit il gawazaet*	passport control

YOU MAY WANT TO SAY...

● I'm here...
   on holiday
   on business

أنا هنا...
فى اجازة
فى مهمة عمل

ana hena...
   fi agaeza
   fi mohimit ªamal

● It's for my own personal use.

للأستخدام الشخصى.

lil istikhdaem ishshakhSee

● I'm an EU citizen.

أنا مواطن من الأتحاد الأوروبى.

ana mowaTin min il itiHad il orobbi

YOU MAY HEAR...

جواز السفر من فضلك.	*ga*waz *issa*far min *faD*lik	Your passport please.
مستندات السفر من فضلك.	*moostana*daet *issa*far min *faD*lak	Your documents please.
ما هو الغرض من الزيارة؟	ma *howa* il *gha*raD min *izzi*yaara	What is the purpose of your visit?
مدة الزيارة هنا قد اية؟	*mow*dit *izzi*yaara *hena* 'ad *ay*	How long are you going to stay here?
من فضلك افتح...	min *faD*lak *ef*taH...	Please open...
الشنطة دى	*ishshan*Ta di	this bag/ suitcase.
شنطة العربية	*shan*Tit il ªara*baya*	the boot.
لازم نفتش السيارة/الأمتعة.	*lae*zim ni*fat*tish *issai*yaara/il *am*teªa	We have to search the car/your luggage.
تعالى معايا من فضلك.	taªala maªaiya min *faD*lak	Come along with me please.

✳ directions

● The easiest way to ask for directions is to name the place you're looking for and add *min faD*lak (to m)/*faD*lik (to f) ('please'). Alternatively you can say 'Where is...?' *fayn...?*

● If you need someone to repeat directions, say 'again, please' *tae*ni min *faD*lak (to m)/*faD*lik (to f).

43

YOU MAY SEE...

ادفع	*idfaª*	push
استعلامات	*isteªlamaet*	information
اوتوبيس	*otobees*	bus
اجذب	*egzib*	pull
تاكسى	*taksi*	taxi
تواليت	*twalit*	toilets
جمرك	*gomrok*	customs
جوازات اخرى	*gawazaet okhra*	other passports
خروج	*khoroog*	exit
دخول	*dokhool*	entrance
سيارات خاصة/الليموزين	*saiyaraat khaaSa/*	private cars/
للأيجار	*limozeen lil iygar*	limousine for hire
شيال	*shaiyael*	porter
مراقبة الجوازات	*moraqabit il gawazaet*	passport control
مكتب تحويل عملة	*maktab taHweel ªomla*	bureau de change
وسط البلد	*wesT il balad*	city centre

YOU MAY WANT TO SAY...

● Excuse me, please.	عن اذنك.	*ªan iznak* (to m)/ *iznik* (to f)
● Where is... the station?	فين... المحطة؟	*fayn...* *il maHaTa*
● Where are...	فين...	*fayn...*
● How do we get to... the airport? the beach?	ازاى اروح... المطار؟ الشاطىء؟	*izzay aroH...* *il maTar* *ishshaaTi'*

Is this the right way to... ?	هل هذا الطريق الصحيح لـ...؟	*hael **haez**a iTTaree' iSSa**HeeH** li...*
Can you show me on the map, please?	ممكن تورينى الطريق على الخريطة؟	***mom**kin tewa**ree**nee iTTaree' ªala il kha**ree**Ta*
Is it far?	بعيد؟	*beªeed*
Is there ... near here? a bank	فى ... قريب من هنا؟ بنك	*fi ... 'oraiyib min **he**na* *bank*
Where is the nearest...?	فين اقرب...؟	*fayn a'rab...*

YOU MAY HEAR...

على طول.	*ªala Tool*	Straight on.
احود... يمين	*e**H**wid... yi**meen***	Turn... right
على طول... لحد الأشارة	*ªala Tool... li**Had** il ish**shaa**ra*	Go on... to the traffic lights
خز اول شارع...	*khod **a**wil shariª...*	Take the first on the...
شمال	*shi**mael***	left
هو... قدام... وراء...	*howa... od**daem**... wara'...*	It's... opposite... behind...
قريب جداً/بعيد جداً.	*'oraiyib/beªeed **ge**dan*	It's very near/far away.

✳ information and tickets

(see **telling the time**, page 20)

Is there a train/ bus/boat to ... today?	فى قطار/أوتوبيس/مركب ل ... النهاردة؟	fi 'aTr/otobees/ markib li ... innaharda
What time is the ... to Amman?	الساعة كام ... ل عمان؟	issaªa kaem ... li amaen
next train	القطار اللى بعد كدة	il 'aTr ili baªd keda
first bus	اول أوتوبيس؟	awil otobees
Do they go often?	بيقوم كل اد إيه؟	biy'oom kol 'addi ay
What time does it arrive?	بيوصل الساعة كام؟	biyowSal issaªa kaem
Do I have to change trains/ buses?	لازم اغير القطار/الأوتوبيس؟	laezim aghaiyar il 'aTr/il otobees
Which platform for...?	اى رصيف...؟	ay raSeef...
Which bus stop for...?	أى محطة...؟	ay maHaTa...
Where can I buy...	منين أشترى...	minayn ashteri...
a ticket?	تذكرة؟	tazkara
One/two tickets to ... please.	تذكرة/تذكرتين ل ... من فضلك.	tazkara/tazkartayn li ... min faDlak (to m)/faDlik (to f)
single	مفرد	mofrad

● return	رايح جاي	*raiyH gaiy*
● I want to reserve...	عايز أحجز...	*ayiz* (m)/*ayza* (f) *aHgiz...*
a seat	كرسي	*korsi*
a cabin	كابينة	*kabeena*
● Is there a supplement?	فى اجرى اضافية؟	*fi ogra iDDafaya*
● Is there a discount for...	فى تخفيض....؟	*fi takhfeeD...*
students?	للطلبة	*liTTalaba*
senior citizens?	للمسنين	*lil mosineen*

YOU MAY HEAR...

بيقوم الساعة...	*biy'oom issa*a...*	It leaves at...
بيوصل الساعة...	*biyowSal issa*a...*	It arrives at...
بيقوم كل عشر دقائق.	*biy'oom kol*ashar da'ye'*	They go every ten minutes.
رصيف رقم...	*raSeef raqam...*	It's platform/pier number four.
يمكنك شراء تذكرة...	*yomkinak shira' tazkara...*	You can buy a ticket...
فى الأوتوبيس/القطار/ المركب	*fi il otobees/ il 'aTr/il markib*	on the bus/ train/boat
ممكن تدفع للسواق	*momkin tedfa*a lil sawa'*	You can pay the driver.
عايز تسافرامتى؟	*ayiz tisaefir emta*	When do you want to travel?

travel and transport

* trains
(see **information and tickets**, page 46)

YOU MAY SEE...

الأمتعة المخزونة	il amteªa il makhzoona	left luggage
الحجز مقدماً	il Hagz mo'adaman	advance booking
السفر/الخروج	issafar/il khoroog	departure/exit
الوصول	il woSool	arrivals
اضراب	iDraab	strike
تأخير	ta'kheer	delay
تزاكر	tazaekir	tickets
تواليت	twalit	toilets
جهة السفر	gehit issafar	destination
خزنات الأمتعة	khazanaet il amteªa	luggage lockers
دخول	dokhool	entrance
رصيف	raSeef	platform
سراير عربات النوم	sarayer ªarabiyaat innowm	couchettes
شباك التذاكر	shibbaek ittazaekir	ticket office
عربة البوفية	ªarabiyat il boofay	restaurant-car
عربة النوم	ªarabiyat innowm	sleeping-car
غرفة الأنتظار	ghorfit il intiZaar	waiting room
قسم الحجز	qesm il Hagz	reservations
قطارات الخطوط الرئيسية	qeTaraat il khoTooT il ra'eesaya	main line trains
قطارات الضواحى	qeTaraat iDDawaaHi	suburban trains
معلومات	maªloomaet	information
مفقودات	mafqoodaet	lost property

YOU MAY WANT TO SAY...

● I'd like a single/ return ticket to ... please.	عايز/عايزة تذكرة رايح/رايح جاي ل ... من فضلك.	^aayiz (m)/^aayza (f) tazkara raiyH/raiyH gaiy li ... min faDlak (to m)/faDlik (to f)
● Are there lifts to the platform?	في اسانسير على الأرصفة؟	fi asansayr ^aala il arSifa
● Does this train go to Mansoura?	هل القطار ده بيروح المنصورة؟	hael il 'aTr da biy'roH il manSoora
● Excuse me, I've reserved...	بعد أذنك انا حجزت...	ba^ad iznak (to m)/ iznik (to f) ana Hagaezt...
that seat a couchette	الكرسي ده السرير ده عربية النوم	ikkorsi da issereer da ^aarabiyaet innowm
● Is this seat taken?	الكرسي ده محجوز؟	ikkorsi da maHgooz?
● May I... open the window? smoke?	ممكن... افتح الشباك؟ ادخن؟	momkin... aftaH ishshibbaek? adakhan
● Where are we?	احنا فين؟	ehna fayn?
● How long does the train stop here?	القطار بيقف هنا قد إيه؟	il 'aTr biyo'af hena 'ad ay
● Can you tell me when we get to Aswan?	ممكن تنبهني لما نوصل أسوان؟	momkin tinabihni lamma newSal aswaan

* buses and coaches
(see **information and tickets,** page 46)

(see **information and tickets,** page 46)

YOU MAY SEE...

الخروج من الباب الأمامى	*il khoroog min il **baeb** il **amae**mi*	exit by the front door
الدخول من الباب الخلفي	*iddo**khool** min il **baeb** il **khal**fi*	enter by the back door
اتوبيس الرحلات البعيدة	*oto**bees** irreHlaet il ba³ee**da***	long-distance coach
برجاء عدم التحدث مع الساثق	*birega' ³adam it taHados ma³ issa'q*	do not talk to the driver
خروج طوارىء	*kho**roog** Tawari'*	emergency exit
دخول	*do**khool***	entrance
محطة اوتوبيس	*maHatit oto**bees***	bus station
ممنوع التدخين	*mamnoo³ ittad**kheen***	no smoking
ممنوع الخروج	*mamnoo³ il kho**roog***	no exit
ممنوع الدخول	*mamnoo³ iddo**khool***	no entry
موقف أوتوبيس	*mawqaf oto**bees***	bus stop

YOU MAY WANT TO SAY...

● Where does the
bus to the town
centre leave
from?

اتوبيس وسط البلد بيقوم
منين؟

*otobees wesT il
balad biy'oom
minayn*

● Does the bus to
the airport leave
from here?

اتوبيس المطار بيقوم
من هنا؟

*otobees il maTar
biy'oom min hena*

● What number
is it?

نمرة كام؟

nemra kaem

● Does this bus go
to...

هل الأوتوبيس ده بيروح...

*hael il otobees da
biyroH...*

  the beach?

الشاطىء؟

ishshaaTi'

  the station?

المحطة؟

il maHaTa

● Which stop is it
for the...

اللى عايز يروح ... ينزل
فين؟

*ili ªayiz yiroH ...
yenzil fayn*

  museum?

المتحف

il matHaf

● Can you tell me
where to get off,
please?

انزل فين من فضلك؟

*anzil fayn min
faDlak (to m)/
faDlik (to f)*

● The next stop,
please.

المحطة اللى جاية من
فضلك؟

*il maHaTa ili gaiya
min faDlak (to m)/
faDlik (to f)*

● Can you open the
doors, please?

ممكن تفتح الأبواب من
فضلك؟

*momkin teftaH il
abwaeb min faDlak
(to m)/faDlik (to f)*

YOU MAY HEAR...

اوتوبيس وسط البلد بيقوم من هنا.	*otobees wesT il balad biy'oom min hena*	The bus to the town centre leaves from here.
اتوبيس رقم سبعة وخمسين بيروح المحطة.	*otobees raqam sabᵃa wi khamseen biyroH il maHaTa*	The number 57 goes to the station.
حا تنزل هنا؟	*Hatenzil hena*	Are you getting off here?
بعد اذنك انا حا انزل هنا.	*baᵃd iznak ana Hanzil hena*	Excuse me, I'm getting off here.
لازم تنزل المحطة اللى جاية.	*laezim tenzil il maHaTa ili gaiya*	You have to get off at the next stop.
فاتتك المحطة.	*fatetak il maHaTa*	You've missed the stop.

* underground
(see **information and tickets,** page 46)

YOU MAY SEE...

الخط رقم ١	*il khaT raqam waHid*	line 1
خروج	*khoroog*	exit
دخول	*dokhool*	entrance
مترو الأنفاق	*metro il anfaq*	underground
معلومات	*maᵃloomaet*	information
ممنوع التدخين	*mamnooᵃ ittadkheen*	no smoking

underground

YOU MAY WANT TO SAY...

- Do you have
  a map of the
  underground?

  عندك خريطة لمترو الأنفاق؟

  ªandak (to m)/
  ªandik (to f)
  *khareeTa
  li metro il anfaq*

- Which line is it
  for the airport?

  اى خط للمطار؟

  ay khaT lil maTaar

- Which stop is it
  for... ?
    the market

  انزل فى اى محطة ل...؟

  السوق

  *anzil fi ay maHaTa
  li...*

  issoo'

- Is this the right
  stop for... ?

  دى محطة...؟

  di maHaTit...

- Does this train go
  to...?

  القطار ده بيروح...؟

  il 'aTr da biyroH...

YOU MAY HEAR...

خط رقم ٢	*khaT raqam itnayn*	It's line number two.
المحطة اللى جاية	*il maHaTa ili gaiya*	It's the next stop.
المحطة اللى فاتت	*il maHaTa ili faetit*	It was the last stop.

travel and transport

53

boats and ferries

✳ boats and ferries
(see **information and tickets**, page 46)

YOU MAY SEE...

رحلات بحرية	*reHlaet baHaraya*	sea cruises
رحلات نهرية	*reHlaet nahraya*	river trips
سترة نجاة	*sotrit nagah*	life jacket
مركب نجاة	*markib nagah*	lifeboat
معدية	*maªadayya*	ferry
موقف مراكب	*mawqif maraekib*	pier
ميناء	*meena*	port

YOU MAY WANT TO SAY...

- I'd like a return ticket to ... please.
عايز/عايزة تذكرة رايح جاى ل ... من فضلك.
ªayiz (m)/*ªayza* (f) *tazkara raiyiH gaiy li ... min faDlak* (to m)/*faDlik* (to f)

- Is there a ferry ... today?
فى معدية ... النهاردة؟
fi maªadayya ... innaharda

- Are there any boat trips?
فى رحلات بالمركب؟
fi raHlaet bil markib

- How long is the cruise?
الرحلة بالمركب قد إيه؟
irreHla bil markib 'addi ay

- What is the sea like today?
البحر كويس النهارده؟
il baHr kwaiyis innaharda

- Is it possible to go out on deck?
هل ممكن نستنى على سطح المركب؟
hael momkin nistanna ªala saTH il markib

travel and transport

54

YOU MAY HEAR...

رحلات المراكب تقوم...	reHlaet il maraekib bit'oom...	Boats go on...
أيام الثلاثاء والجمعة	ayaem ittalaet wil gom^aa	Tuesdays and Fridays
يوم بعد يوم	yowm ba^ad yowm	every other day
البحر...	il baHr...	The sea is...
هادىء	haedi	calm
هائج	haeyig	choppy

✳ air travel
(see **information and tickets**, page 46)

YOU MAY SEE...

استلام الحقائب	istilaem il Haqa'ib	luggage reclaim
الأمن	il 'amn	security
الرحلات الدولية	il reHlaet iddawlaya	international departures
السفر	issafar	departures
الصعود	iSSo^aood	boarding
تأجير سيارات	ta'geer saiyaraat	car hire
تأخير	ta'kheer	delay
جمرك	gomrok	customs
صالة السفر	Saalit issafar	departure lounge
مراقبة الجوازات	moraqabit il gawazaet	passport control
مطار	maTaar	airport
مكتب التسجيل	maktab ittasgeel	check-in
وصول	woSool	arrivals

air travel

YOU MAY WANT TO SAY...

- I'd like a return ticket to... please.
  عايز/عايزة تذكرة رايح جاي ... من فضلك.
  ^aayiz (m)/^aayza (f) tazkara raiyiH gaiy li ... min faDlak (to m)/faDlik (to f)

- I want to change my ticket.
  عايز/عايزة اغير التذكرة.
  ^aayiz (m)/^aayza (f) aghaiyar ittazkara

- I want to cancel my ticket.
  عايز/عايزة الغى التذكرة.
  ^aayiz (m)/^aayza (f) alghee ittazkara

- What time do I/we have to check in?
  التسجيل الساعة كام؟
  ittasgeel issa^aa kaem

- Is there a delay?
  فى تاخير؟
  fi ta'khyeer

- Which gate is it?
  إى بوابة؟
  ay bawaeba

- My luggage hasn't arrived.
  شنطى ما وصلتش.
  shonaTi mawaSalitsh

- Is there a bus/ train to the centre of town?
  فى اتوبيس/قطارلوسط البلد؟
  fi otobees/'aTr li wesT il balad

WORDS TO LISTEN OUT FOR...

اخر نداء	akhir nidae'	last call
بوابة	bawaeba	gate
تاخير	ta'kheer	delay
رحلة	reHla	flight
ملغى	malghi	cancelled
نداء	nida'	call

56

* taxis

(see **directions**, page 43)

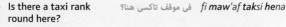

- Is there a taxi rank round here?

  فى موقف تاكسى هنا؟

  fi maw'af taksi hena

- Can you order me a taxi...

  ممكن احجز تاكسى...

  momkin aHgiz taksi...

  immediately

  فورآ

  fawran

  for tomorrow at nine o'clock

  لبكرة الساعة التاسعة

  li bokra issaªa tesªa

- To this address, please.

  على العنوان ده من فضلك.

  ªala il ªenwaen da min faDlak (to m)/ faDlik (to f)

- How much will it cost?

  حا يتكلف قد إيه؟

  Ha yetkalif 'addi ay

- Please use the meter.

  استعمل العداد من فضلك.

  istaªmil il ªadaed min faDlak (to m)/ faDlik (to f)

- Stop here, please.

  قف هنا من فضلك.

  qef hena min faDlak (to m)/faDlik (to f)

- Can you wait for me, please?

  ممكن تنتظرنى من فضلك.

  momkin tantaZerni min faDlak (to m)/ faDlik (to f)

- I think there's a mistake.

  فى خطأ فى الحساب.

  fi khaTa' fil Hisaeb

- Keep the change.

  خللى الباقى.

  khali il bae'ee

- Can you give me a receipt, please?

  ممكن وصل من فضلك؟

  momkin waSl min faDlak (to m)/ faDlik (to f)

hiring cars and bicycles

YOU MAY HEAR...

على بعد عشرة كيلومتر.	ⁱala boⁱd ⁱashara keelometr	It's ten kilometres away.
الحساب حا يكون سبعين درهم تقريباً.	il Hisaeb Haiykoon sabaⁱeen derham ta'reeban	It'll cost about 70 dirham.
في أجرة إضافية على...	fi ogra iDafaya ⁱala...	There's a supplement for...
كل شنطة	kol shanTa	each suitcase

* hiring cars and bicycles

YOU MAY WANT TO SAY...

● I'd like to hire...	عايز/عايزة أأجر...	ⁱayiz (m)/ⁱayza (f) 'a'aggar...
two bicycles	عجلتين	ⁱagaltayn
a small car	عربية صغيرة	ⁱarabaya Soghaiyara
an automatic car	عربية اوتوماتيك	ⁱarabaya otomatik
● For one day	لمدة يوم واحد	limodit yowm waHid
● For...	لمدة...	limodit...
a week	اسبوع	izbooⁱ
two weeks	اسبوعين	izbooⁱayn
● Until...	لغاية...	lighaiyit...
Friday	يوم الجمعة	yowm il gomⁱa
the 17th August	يوم سبعة عشر اغسطس	yowm sabⁱatashar aghosTos

- How much is it...   بكام...   *bikaem...*
  per day?   فى اليوم؟   *fil yowm*
  per week?   فى الأسبوع؟   *fil izboo^a*

- Is kilometrage/ mileage included?   السعر يشمل المسافة المقطوعة؟   *is se^ar yashmal il masaefa il maqToo^aa*

- Is insurance included?   السعر يشمل التأمين؟   *is se^ar yashmal il ta'meen*

- Does the insurance cover two drivers?   هل التأمين يشمل شخصين؟   *hael it ta'meen yashmal shakhSayn*

- Is there a deposit?   فى عربون؟   *fi ^aarboon*

- Can you put the saddle up/down, please?   ممكن تعلى/ توطى الكرسى من فضلك؟   *momkin te^aali/ tewaTi il korsi min faDlak (to m)/ faDlik (to f)*

YOU MAY HEAR...

اى نوع من العربيات/ الدراجات تحب؟	*ay now^a min il ^aarabiyaat/il ^aagal teHeb*	What kind of car/bicycle do you want?
لمدة قد إيه؟	*limodit 'addi ay*	For how long?
من...	*meen...*	Who's...
السائق الأساسى؟	*issawae' il asaesi*	the main driver?
السائق الثانى؟	*issawae' ittaeni*	the second driver?
رخصة القيادة من فضلك؟	*rokhSit il qiyaeda min faDlak*	Your driving licence, please.

عايز تأمين إضافي؟	*ayiz ta'**meen** iDaa**fi*	Do you want extra insurance?
من فضلك املا خزان بنزين العربية قبل ما ترجعها.	min **faD**lak emla kha**za**en ben**zeen** il *ara**bay**a 'abl ma **tra**ga*ha	Please return the car with a full tank.
من فضلك رجع العربية/العجلة قبل الساعة السادسة.	min **faD**lak **ra**ga*i il *ara**bay**a/il *a**gal**a 'abl is**sa**a seta	Please return the car/bicycle before six o'clock.

✳ driving
(see **directions**, page 43)

YOU MAY SEE... 👁

الأولوية لليمين	il awla**way**a lil yi**meen**	priority to the right
التزم اليمين	il**ta**zim il yi**meen**	keep right
السرعة القصوى	is**sor**a il **qoS**wa	maximum speed limit
الطريق مغلق	iT**Ta**ree' **mogh**laq	road closed
أحزر	e**H**zar	caution
انحناء خطر	in**Hi**na' **kha**Tar	dangerous bend
اوتوستراد	otos**traad**	motorway
إطفيء المحرك	e**T**fi' il mo**Har**rik	switch your engine off
جراج	ga**raaj**	garage
خطر	**kha**Tar	danger
طريق ذو إتجاه واحد	**Ta**ree' zoo iti**gaeh** wa**Hid**	one-way street

عبور مشاة	ªoboor mooshaeh	pedestrian crossing
قف	qef	stop
محطة بنزين	maHaTit benzeen	petrol station
مدرسة	madrassa	school
مشاة	mooshaeh	pedestrians
مزلقان	mazla'aen	level crossing
ممر للدراجات	mamar liddarragaat	bicycle path
ممنوع الدخول	mamnooª iddokhool	no entry
ممنوع الركن	mamnooª irrakn	no parking
موقف سيارات	mawqaf saiyaraat	car park
نقطة اسعاف أولى	no'Tit isaªaef awali	first-aid post
نهاية الأوتوستراد	nihayit il otostraad	end of motorway
هدىء	hadi'	slow
هدىء السرعة	hadi' issorªa	drive slowly
وسط البلد	wesT il balad	town centre
وسط المدينة	wesT il madeena	city centre
محطة خدمة	maHaTit khedma	service station
اعطى الأولوية	aªTi il awlawaya	give way
اشغال طرق	ashghael Toro'	road works
ممنوع التجاوز	mamnooª ittagawiz	no overtaking
استعمل الأضواء الأمامية	istaªmil il aDwa' il amaemaya	use headlights

YOU MAY WANT TO SAY...

- Where is the
  nearest petrol
  station?

  فين اقرب محطة بترول؟

  fayn a'rab maHaTit
  benzeen

- Fill it up with...

  املء العربية...

  emla il ªarabaya

  petrol

  بنزين

  benzeen

  diesel

  ديزل

  deezil

  L.E. 20 worth
  of petrol,
  please.

  بعشرين جنية بنزين
  من فضلك

  bi ªishreen ginay
  benzeen min
  faDlak (to
  m)/*faDlik*
  (to f)

  30 litres of
  super
  unleaded,
  please.

  ثلاثين لتر سوبر من
  فضلك

  talaeteen litr
  sooper min
  faDlak (to
  m)/*faDlik*
  (to f)

- A can of oil,
  please.

  علبة زيت من فضلك.

  ªelbit zayt min
  faDlak (to m)/
  faDlik (to f)

- Can you check
  the tyre pressure,
  please?

  ممكن تكشف على ضغط
  العجل من فضلك؟

  momkin tekshif
  ªala DaghT il ªagal
  min faDlak (to m)/
  faDlik (to f)

- Can you change
  the tyre, please?

  ممكن تغير الكوتش من
  فضلك؟

  momkin teghaiyar
  il kawetch min
  faDlak (to m)/
  faDlik (to f)

- Where is the air,
  please?

  فين محبس الهواء من
  فضلك؟

  fayn maHbas il
  hawa min faDlak
  (to m)/*faDlik* (to f)

mechanical problems

YOU MAY HEAR...

اى خدمة؟	*ay khed*ma	Can I help you?
عايز قدامة؟	ªay*iz 'addi ay*	How much do you want?
المفتاح من فضلك.	*il mof*taeH *min faD*lak	The key, please.

✳ mechanical problems

YOU MAY WANT TO SAY...

• My car has broken down.	العربية عطلت.	*il ªaraba*ya ªe*Tlit*
• I've run out of petrol.	البنزين خلص.	*il ben*zeen khe*liS*
• I have a puncture.	فى خرم فى الكوتش.	*fi khorm fil ka*wetch*
• Can you telephone a garage?	ممكن تتصل بجراج؟	*mom*kin teta*Sil biga*raaj*
• Do you do repairs?	بتصلح سيارات؟	*bitSa*laH saiya*raat*
• The ... doesn't work.	ال ... ما بيشتغلش.	*il ... ma biyeshtaghal*sh*
• Is it serious?	العطل كبير؟	*il ª*oTl ki*beer*
• Can you repair it today?	ممكن تصلحها النهارده؟	*mom*kin teSalaH*ha inna*har*da*
• When will it be ready?	حا تجهز أمتى؟	*Hateg*haz em*ta*
• How much will it cost?	حا تتكلف كام؟	*Hatetka*lif *kaem*

travel and transport

63

car parts

YOU MAY HEAR...

إيه سبب العطل؟	ay *sabab* il *°oTl*	What's wrong with it?
ما عنديش قطع الغيار المطلوبة.	ma°an*deesh* qeTa° il *ghiyar* il maT*looba*	I don't have the necessary parts.
لازم نطلب قطع الغيار من الوكيل.	laezim *noTlob* qeTa° il ghiyar min il wa*keel*	I'll have to order the parts from the distributor.
تعالى يوم الثلاثاء اللى جاى.	ta°ala *yowm* itta*laet* ili *gaiy*	Come back next Tuesday.
حا تكون جاهزة...	Hat*koon* gah*za*...	It'll be ready...
فى خلال ساعة	fi khi*lael* sa°a	in an hour
يوم الأثنين	*yowm* il it*nayn*	on Monday
الحساب حا يكون...	il Hi*saeb* Haiy*koon*...	It'll cost...

* car parts

YOU MAY WANT TO SAY...

accelerator	دواسة البنزين	da*wae*sit il ben*zeen*
back tyre	الكاوتش الخلفى	il ka*wetch* il *khal*fi
battery	البطارية	il ba*Tara*ya
bonnet	غطاء المحرك	gha*Ta* il mo*Harrik*
boot	الشنطة	ish*shan*Ta
brakes	الفرامل	il fa*raamil*
carburettor	الكاربيراتور	il karbi*ray*tor

64

engine	المحرك	*il moHarrik*
exhaust pipe	انبوبة العادم	*anboobit il ªaedem*
fanbelt	حزام المروحة	*Hizaem il marwaHa*
front tyre	الكاوتش الأمامي	*il kawetch il amaemi*
fuel gauge	مؤشر مضخة البنزين	*mo'ashir maDakhit il benzeen*
gear box	علبة التروس	*ªelbit ittoroos*
gears	التروس	*ittoroos*
headlights	الكشافات الأمامية	*il kashafaet il amaemaya*
ignition	مفتاح المحرك	*moftaeH il moHarrik*
indicator	المؤشر الجانبي	*il mo'ashir il gaenibi*
radiator	خزان المياة	*khazaen il maiya*
rear lights	الكشافات الخلفية	*il kashafaet il khalfaya*
reversing lights	كشافات الرجوع	*kashafaet irrogooª*
side lights	الكشافات الجانبية	*il kashafaet il gaenibaya*
spare tyre	فردة استبن	*farda istebn*
spark plugs	فيش الصمامات	*fayesh iSSamamaat*
starter motor	مشغل المحرك	*moshaghil il moHarrik*
steering wheel	عجلة القيادة	*ªagalit il qiyaeda*
windscreen	الزجاج الأمامي	*izzogaeg il amaemi*

* bicycle parts

YOU MAY WANT TO SAY...

back light	الكشاف الخلفى	il kashaef il khalfi
chain	السلسلة	issilsila
frame	إطار العجلة	iTar il ªagala
front light	الكشاف الأمامى	il kashaef il amaemi
gears	مسننات التحكم	mowsaninaet ittaHakom
handlebars	الجدون	il gadown
inner tube	أنبوبة داخلية	ambooba dakhalaya
pump	مضخة	maDakha
saddle	كرسى/سرج	korsi/sarg
spokes	اسلاك العجلة	aslaek il ªagala
tyre	كاوتش	kawetch
valve	صمامة	Samaama
wheel	عجلة	ªagala
wheel rim	حرف العجلة	Harf il ªagala

booking in advance	69
checking in	73
hotels, B&Bs and hostels	74
camping	77
requests and queries	78
problems and complaints	80
checking out	83
self-catering/second homes	84

accommodation

● There is a wide range of accommodation available throughout Arab countries. Each country has its own system of hotel accreditation, some following the European star system and others regulated by the government.

YOU MAY SEE...

الأستقبال	il istiqbael	reception
البدرون	il badrown	basement
الدور الأرضى	iddowr il arDi	ground floor
الدور الأول/	iddowr il awil/il dowr	first floor/second
الدور الثانى	itaeni	floor
الصالون	iSSalown	lounge
المطعم	il maTᵃam	restaurant
أسانسير	asansayr	lift
اسعار الغرف	asᵃaar il ghoraf	charge, tariff
بيت شباب	bayt shebaeb	youth hostel
تواليت (رجال)	twalit (rigael)	toilets (male)
تواليت (سيدات)	twalit (sayedaet)	toilets (female)
جراج	garaaj	garage
خدمات الغرف	khadamaet il ghoraf	room service
خروج (طوارىء)	khoroog (Tawari')	(emergency) exit
دش	dosh	showers
زبالة	zibaela	rubbish
غرف للأيجار	ghoraf lil igar	rooms (vacancies)
غرفة التلفزيون	ghorfit ittelevisyown	television room
غرفة الطعام	ghorfit iTTaᵃam	dining room
غرفة مع الفطار	ghorfa maᵃ ilifTar	bed and breakfast
كامل العدد	kaemil il ᵃadad	full
كهرباء	kahrabba	electricity
مياة صالحة للشرب	maiya SalHa li shorb	drinking water

معسكر	*mow^aaskar*	campsite
مغسلة	*maghsalla*	laundry
ممنوع إقامة الخيام	*mamnoo^a iqaamit il khiyaem*	no camping
من فضلك رن الجرس	*min faDlak rin il garas*	please ring the bell
هوتيل	*hotel*	hotel
هوتيل خمس نجوم	*hotel khamas negoom*	five-star hotel

* booking in advance

(see **telephones**, page 150; the **internet,** page 152)

● When booking accommodation, be aware that local taxes will usually be added on to the advertised price. It's also worth noting that in many parts of the Middle East an unmarried man and woman will not be allowed to share a room.

YOU MAY WANT TO SAY...

● Do you have a ... room?	عندك غرفة ... للإيجار؟	*^aandak* (to m)/ *^aandik* (to f) *ghorfa ... lil igar*
family	للعائلات	*^aa'ilaet*
twin-bedded	بسريرين	*bisirirayn*
single	سرير مفرد	*sereer mofrad*
double	سرير مزدوج	*sereer mozdawag*
adjoining rooms	غرفتين باب مشترك	*ghorfatayn bibaeb moshtarak*

accommodation

69

booking in advance

Do you have...	...عندك	^a*andak* (to m)/ ^a*andik* (to f)...
space for a tent?	مكان لخيمة؟	*makaen likhae*ma
I'd like to rent...	عايز ... للأيجار	^a*ayiz* (m)/^a*ayza* (f) ...*liligar*
an apartment	شقة	*sha'a*
a house	بيت	*bayt*
For...	...لمدة	*limodit...*
one night	ليلة واحدة	*layla waH*da
two nights	ليلتين	*layl*tayn
a week	أسبوع	*izboo*^a
From ... to...	... إلى ... من	*min ... ila...*
with...	...بال	*bil...*
bath	بانيو	*ban*yo
shower	الدش	*iddosh*
It's a two-person tent.	خيمة لشخصين.	*khay*ma li *shakhSayn*
How much is it...	...بكام	*bikaem...*
per night?	فى الليلة؟	*filay*la
per week?	فى الأسبوع؟	*fil izboo*^a
Is breakfast included?	هل يشمل الأفطار؟	*hael yash*mal *ilifTaar*
Is there...	...فى	*fi...*
a reduction for children?	تخفيض للأطفال؟	*takhfeeD lilaTfaal*
a single room supplement?	سعر إضافى للغرفة المفردة؟	*se*^a*r iDaafi lilghorfa il mofrada*
wheelchair access?	مدخل لكراسى المعوقين؟	*madkhal likaraesi il mow*^a*awaqeen*

- Do you have...

  anything cheaper?

  a larger room?

  air conditioning?

  satellite TV?

  a website?

- Can I pay by...

  credit card?

  travellers' cheques?

- Can I book online?

- What's the address?

- What's your email address?

- How do I find you?

- Can you recommend anywhere else?

عندك...

غرفة ارخص؟

غرفة اكبر؟

تكييف هواء؟

تلفزيون بالساتلايت؟

وب سايت؟

ممكن ادفع ب...

كرت الأتمان؟

شيكات سياحية؟

ممكن الحجز بالأنترنت؟

العنوان إيه؟

ما هو عنوانك الألكتروني؟

ابحث عنك فين؟

هل ممكن تنصحنى الاقى مكان تانى؟

andak (to m)/
andik (to f)...

ghorfa arkhaS

ghorfa akbar

takyeef hawa

televisyown bil satilait

websait

momkin adfa bi...

kart il 'i'timaen

shikaet siyaHaya

momkin il Hagz bil internet

*il *enwaen ay*

*ma howa *enwaenak (to m)/*enwaenik (to f) il elektrowni*

*abHas *anak (to m)/anik (to f) fayn*

hael momkin tinSaHni ala'i makaen taeni

booking in advance

ممكن اساعدك؟	*momkin as*ᵃ*adak*	Can I help you?
حا تزورونا امتى؟	*Hatzooroona emta*	When will you visit us?
لمدة كام ليلة؟	*limodit kaem layla*	For how many nights?
عدد الأفراد؟	ᵃ*adad ilafraad*	For how many people?
غرفة بسرير ولا بسريرين؟	*ghorfa bi sereer wala bi sereerayn*	Single or double room?
عايز سرير مزدوج؟	ᵃ*ayiz sereer mozdawag*	Do you want a double bed?
بالحمام؟	*bilHamaem*	With a bathroom?
الخيمة لكام فرد؟	*il khayma likaem fard*	The tent sleeps how many people?
اسمك إيه من فضلك؟	*ismak ay min faDlak*	What's your name, please?
عندك بطاقة ائتمان؟	ᵃ*andak biTa'it 'i'timaen*	Do you have a credit card?
السعر ربعمائة جنية فى الليلة ويشمل الفطار.	*isse*ᵃ*r rob*ᵃ *meet ginee filayla wi yeshmal ilfiTar*	It's 400 L.E. (Egyptian Pounds) per night, including breakfast.
اسفة الهوتيل كامل العدد.	*asfa il hotel kaemil il* ᵃ*adad*	I'm sorry, the hotel is full.

accommodation

72

* checking in

YOU MAY WANT TO SAY...

- I have a reservation for... | انا حجزت غرفة... | ana Hagazt ghorfa...
  - tonight | الليلة | illayla
  - two nights | ليلتين | layltayn
  - a week | اسبوع | izbooª
- It's in the name of... | بأسم... | bism...
- Here's my passport. | جواز سفرى. | gawaez safari
- I'm paying by credit card. | حا ادفع بكارت الأتمان. | Hadfaª bikart il 'i'timaen

YOU MAY HEAR...

هل حجزت غرفة/مكان؟	hael Hagazt ghorfa/ makaen	Have you reserved a room/space?
لمدة كام ليلة؟	limowdit kaem layla	For how many nights?
اسمك إيه؟	ismak ay	What's your name?
طريقة الدفع؟	Taree'it iddafa	How are you going to pay?

hotels, B&Bs and hostels

REGISTRATION CARD INFORMATION...

الاسم	first name
اسم العائلة	surname
العنوان/الشارع/الرقم	home address/street/number
الرقم البريدي	postcode
الجنسية	nationality
الوظيفة	occupation
تاريخ الميلاد	date of birth
محل الميلاد	place of birth
رقم جواز السفر	passport number
مسافر من	coming from
مسافر إلى	going to
التاريخ	date
الأمضاء	signature

* hotels, B&Bs and hostels

YOU MAY WANT TO SAY...

● Where can I park?	ارکن العربية فين؟	*arkin il ªarabaya fayn*
● Can I see the room please?	ممكن اشوف الغرفة من فضلك؟	*momkin ashoof il ghorfa min faDlak* (to m)/*faDlik* (to f)
● Is breakfast included?	يشمل الفطار؟	*yeshmal il fiTaar*
● What time is breakfast?	الفطار الساعة کام؟	*il fiTaar issaªa kaem*

74

hotels, B&Bs and hostels

- Do you have...   عندك...   ^aandak (to m)/^aandik (to f)...

    a room overlooking the sea?   غرفة على... البحر؟   ghorfa ^aala il baHr

    a garden?   الجنينة؟   il ginayna

    a swimming pool?   حمام السباحة؟   Hamaem issibaHa

    a bigger room?   غرفة أكبر؟   ghorfa akbar

    a cot for the baby?   سرير للأطفال؟   sereer lil aTfaal

- Where is...   فين...   fayn...

    the dining room?   غرفة الطعام؟   ghorfit iTTa^aam

- Is there...   فى ...   fi...

    24-hour room service?   خدمة الغرف اربعة و عشرين ساعة؟   khedmit il ghoraf arba^aa wi ^aishreen sa^aa

    an internet connection?   وصلة انترنت؟   waSlit internet

    a business centre here?   مركز خدمة رجال الأعمال؟   markaz khedmit rigael il a^amael

YOU MAY HEAR...

موقف السيارات...	mowqaf issaiyaraat...	The car park is...
تحت الهوتيل	taHt il hotel	under the hotel
فى اول الشارع	fi awil ishshari^a	up the road
مفيش غرف فاضية الليلة.	mafeesh ghorfa faDya il ayla	I'm afraid we don't have any rooms available tonight.

accommodation

75

ممكن نغير الغرفة بكرة.	*momkin neghaiyar il ghorfa bokra*	We might be able to change your room tomorrow.
يشمل/لا يشمل الفطار.	*yeshmal/la yeshmal il fiTaar*	Breakfast is/isn't included.
الفطار من الساعة ... للساعة...	*il fiTaar min issaªa ... lissaªa...*	Breakfast is from ... to...
اتفضل غرفة الطعام من هنا.	*itfaDal ghorfit iTTaªam min hena*	Follow me, I'll show you where the dining room/ bar is.
خدمة الغرف متوفرة من ... للساعة...	*khedmit il ghoraf mowtawafera min issaªa ...lissaªa...*	There's room service from ... to...
أيوة عندنا خدمة الغرف أربعة و عشرين ساعة.	*aiywa ªandena khedmit il ghoraf arba-ªa wi ªishreen saªa*	Yes, there's 24-hour room service.
فى وصلة انترنت...	*fi waSlit internet...*	There's an internet connection...
فى مركز رجال الأعمال.	*fi markaz rigael il aªmael*	in the business centre.
فى الغرفة.	*fil ghorfa*	in your room.

* camping

(see **directions**, page 43)

- Is there a
  campsite round
  here?

  فى معسكر هنا؟   *fi mowªaskar hena*

- Can we camp
  here?

  ممكن نعسكر هنا؟   *momkin neªaskar hena*

- It's a two/four
  person tent.

  الخيمة تساع شخصين/أربع أشخاص.   *il khayma tisaeª shakhSayn/arbaª ashkhaS*

- Where are...

  فين...   *fayn...*

    the toilets?   التواليت؟   *ittwalit*
    the showers?   الحمام؟   *il Hamaem*
    the dustbins?   صناديق الزبالة؟   *Sanadiq izzibaela*

- Do we pay extra
  for the showers?

  السعر يشمل/الدش؟   *isseªr yeshmal iddosh*

- Is this drinking
  water?

  المياة صالحة للشرب؟   *il maiya SaliHa lishshorb*

- Is there an electric
  point?

  فى فيشة كهرباء؟   *fi feeshit kahrabba*

الاقرب معسكر...   *a'rab moªaskar...*   The nearest
campsite is...

على بعد خمسة كيلومتر من هنا.   *ala boªd khamsa keelometr min hena*   five kilometres
away.

accommodation

77

requests and queries

فى القرية اللى بعدنا	fil *qarya ili ba*a*dena*	in the next village.
عندك خريطة؟	a*andak khareeTa*	Have you got a map?
ممنوع الخيم هنا.	mamnoo*a il khayem hena*	You can't camp here.
الدش ببلاش.	iddosh bibalaesh	The showers are free.
السعر ... للدش الواحد.	isse*a*r ... lil dosh il waHid	It's ... for a shower.
الفيشة هناك.	il feesha hinaek	The electricity point is over there.

✳ requests and queries

YOU MAY WANT TO SAY...

- Are there any messages for me? — فى رسائل علشانى؟ — fi resae'il a*alashaeni*

- Is there a fax for me? — فى فاكس علشانى؟ — fi faks a*alashaeni*

- I'm expecting... — انا فى نتظار... — ana fi intiZar...
  - a phone call — مكالمة تليفونية — mowkalma tilifownaya
  - a fax — فاكس — faks

- Can I... — ممكن... — momkin...
  - use the hotel safe? — استعمل خزنة الهوتيل؟ — asta*a*mil khaznit il hotel
  - put it on my room bill? — ضيفها على الحساب؟ — Defha a*alal Hisaeb

accommodation

78

- Can you... | ممكن... | *momkin...*
  - give me my things from the safe? | أخذ حاجتى من الخزنة؟ | *aekhod Hagti min il khazna*
  - wake me up at eight o'clock? | تصحينى الساعة تمانية؟ | *teSaHeeni issaªa tamanya*
  - order me a taxi? | تطلب لى تاكسى؟ | *toTlobli taxi*
  - come back later, please? | تعالى كمان شوية من فضلك؟ | *taªala kamaen showaiya min faDlak* (to m)/*faDlik* (to f)

- Do you have... | عندك... | *ªandak* (to m)/ *ªandik* (to f)...
  - a babysitting service? | جليسة اطفال؟ | *galeesit aTfaal*
  - a baby alarm? | جهاز انزار للأطفال؟ | *gehaez inzaar lil aTfaal*

- Can I have an extra... | ممكن ... كمان؟ | *momkin ... kamaen*
  - blanket? | بطانية | *baTanaya*
  - pillow? | مخدة | *makhadda*

- I need... | عايز / عايزة... | *ªayiz* (m)/*ªayza* (f)
  - an adaptor | محول الكهرباء | *mowHawil kahraba*

- I've lost my key. | مفتاحى ضاع. | *moftaeHi Daª*

- I've left my key in the room. | نسيت المفتاح فى الغرفة. | *neseet il moftaeH fil ghorfa*

problems and complaints

YOU MAY HEAR...

فى رسالة فاكس علشانك.	fi resaela/faks ªalashaenak	There's a message/fax for you.
لا مفيش رسائل علشانك.	la mafeesh resae'il ªalashaenak	No, there are no messages for you.
هل تريد مكالمة إيقاظ؟	hael toreed mokalmit eeqaaZ	Do you want a wake up call?
الساعة كام؟	issaªa kaem	(For) what time?
عايز جليسة أطفال الساعة كام؟	ªayiz galeesit aTfaal isaªa kaem	When do you want a babysitter for?
لحظة من فضلك.	laHZa min faDlik	Just a moment, please.

* problems and complaints

YOU MAY WANT TO SAY...

- Excuse me.

  بعد إذنك baªd iznak (to m)/
  iznik (to f)

- The room is... الغرفة... il ghorfa...

  too hot حار جداً Har gedan

  too cold برد جداً bard gedan

  too small صغيرة جداً Soghaiyara gedan

  too noisy دوشة جداً dawsha gedan

  very dirty وسخة جداً weskha gedan

- There isn't any... مفيش... mafeesh...

  toilet paper ورق تواليت wara' twalit

  hot water ماية سخنة maiya sokhna

  electricity كهرباء kahrabba

problems and complaints

English	Arabic	Transliteration
There aren't any...	...مفيش	mafeesh...
towels	فوط	fowaT
soap	صابون	Saboon
I can't...	...مش عارف	mish *arif (m)/*arfa (f)...
open the window	افتح الشباك	aftaH ishshibaek
turn the tap off	اقفل الحنفية	a'fil ilHanafaya
switch on the TV	افتح التليفزيون	aftaH il televisyown
The bed is uncomfortable.	السرير مش مريح.	issereer mish moreeH
The bathroom is dirty.	الحمام مش نظيف.	il Hamaem mish naDeef
The toilets are dirty.	التواليت مش نظيف.	ittwalit mish naDeef
The toilet doesn't flush.	السيفون عطلان.	issifown *aTlaan
The washbasin is blocked.	الحوض مسدود.	il HowD masdood
The light/key doesn't work.	مفتاح النور مكسور.	moftaeH/innoor maksoor
The microwave/remote control is broken.	الريموت عطلان.	il microwayv/irremowt *aTlaan
The shower is not working.	الدش عطلان.	iddosh *aTlaan
There's a smell of gas.	فى رائحة غاز.	fi reeHit ghaez

accommodation

81

problems and complaints

- The washing machine is leaking. — الغسالة بتنزل مايه. — *il ghasaela bitnazil maiya*

- There are insects in the room. — فى حشرات فى الغرفة. — *fi Hasharaat fil ghorfa*

- Can you solve this problem? — ممكن تحل المشكلة دى؟ — *momkin teHel il moshkila di*

- I want to change the room. — عايز/عايزة اغير الغرفة؟ — *ªayiz (m)/ªayza (f) aghaiyar il ghorfa*

- I want to see the manager. — عايز/عايزة اقابل المدير. — *ªayiz (m)/ªayza (f) a'aabil il modeer*

YOU MAY HEAR...

لحظة من فضلك.	*laHZa min faDlak/ faDlik*	Just a moment, please.
طبعآ.	*Tabªan*	Of course.
حا اصلحها لك بكرة.	*HaSalaH-ha lak bokra*	I'll fix it for you tomorrow.
انا اسف/اسفة مش ممكن النهاردة.	*ana aesif (m)/asfa (f) mish momkin inaharda*	I'm sorry, it's not possible today.
انا اسف/اسفة مفيش حاجة أقدر أعملها.	*ana aesif (m)/asfa (f) mafeesh Haga a'dar aªmelha*	I'm sorry, there's nothing I can do.

accommodation

82

✳ checking out

YOU MAY WANT TO SAY... 💬

● The bill, please.
الفاتورة من فضلك.
il faToora min faDlak (to m)/ *faDlik* (to f)

● I'd like to...
أنا عايز/عايزة...
ana ªayiz (m)/*ªayza* (f)...

   pay the bill and check out.
أدفع الفاتورة
adfaª il faToora

   stay another night.
ليلة كمان
layla kamaen

● What time is check out?
المغادرة تنتهى الساعة كام؟
il moghadra tintehi issaªa kaem

● Can I...
ممكن...
momkin...

   have a late check out?
تأخير ميعاد المغادرة
*ta'kheer mi*ªaed il moghadra*

   leave my luggage here?
سيب الشنط هنا؟
aseeb ishshanTa hena

● What does this mean?
مش فاهم/فاهمة يعنى إيه؟
mish faehim (m)/ *fahma* (f) *yaªnni ay*

● There's a mistake in the bill.
فى خطأ فى الفاتورة.
fi khaTa' fil faToora

● I/We've had a great time here.
قضيت /قضينا وقت رائع هنا.
'aDaet/'aDaena wa't raªeª hena

self-catering/second homes

YOU MAY HEAR...

المغادرة الساعة...	*il moghadra issaªa...*	Check out is at...
يمكنك البقاء فى الغرفة لغاية ...	*yemkinak albaqa' fil ghorfa lighaiyit...*	You can have the room till...
كام شنطة؟	*kaem shanTa*	How many bags?
سيبهم هنا.	*sebhom hena*	Leave them here.
الشيال حا يحطهم فى المخزن.	*ishshaiyael hayeHoTo-hom fil makhzan*	The porter will put them in the storeroom.
نتمنى تزورونا تانى.	*natamana toozooroona taeni*	We hope you will visit us again.

✷ self-catering/second homes
(see **problems and complaints**, page 80)

YOU MAY WANT TO SAY...

- I've rented...
  a villa
  an apartment

  انا اجرت...
  فيللا
  شقة

  ana aggart...
  villa
  sha'a

- My name is...

  اسمى...

  ismi...

- Can you give me the key, please?

  المفتاح من فضلك؟

  il moftaeH min faDlak (to m)/ faDlik (to f)

- Where is...
  the fusebox?

  فين...
  علبة صمامات الكهرباء؟

  fayn...
  ªelbit Samaamaat il kahrabba

accommodation

84

self-catering/second homes

- How does the ... work?
  كيف يعمل...
  kayf ya^amal...

  cooker
  البوتاجاز؟
  il botagaez

  boiler
  السخان؟
  issakhaen

- Is there...
  فى...
  fi...

  air conditioning?
  تكييف هواء؟
  takyeef hawa

  another gas bottle?
  انبوبة بوتاجاز تانية؟
  anboobit botagaez tanya

- Are there...
  فى...
  fi...

  any more blankets?
  بطاطين كمان؟
  baTaTeen kamaen

  any shops round here?
  محلات فى المنطقة؟
  maHalaet fil manTe'a

- Where do I/we put the rubbish?
  ارمى الزبالة فين؟
  armi izzibaela fayn

- When do they come to clean?
  بينظفوا امتى؟
  biynaDafoo emta

- Can I borrow...
  ممكن استلف...
  momkin astelif...

  a screwdriver?
  مفك؟
  mifak

- We need...
  عايزين...
  ^aayzeen...

  a plumber
  سباك
  sabaek

  an electrician
  كهربائى
  kahrobae'i

- How can I contact you?
  أتصل بك إزاى؟
  ataSil beek (to m)/ beeki (to f) izzay

- What shall we do with the key when we leave?
  أسيب المفتاح فين قبل المغادرة؟
  aseeb il moftaeH fayn abl il moghadra

YOU MAY HEAR...

علبة صمامات الكهرباء /المحبس هنا.	*elbit Samaamaat il kahrabba/il maHbas hena	The fusebox/ stopcock is here.
تعليمات الأستخدام بجانب البوتاجاز/السخان.	ta*limaet ilistikhdaem bigaenib il botagaez/ issakhaen	The instructions are by the cooker/ boiler.
يشتغل كده.	biyishtagal keda	It works like this.
اضغط على الزرار ده.	iDghaT *ala izzoorar da	Press this button/ switch.
فى بطاطين/مخدات زياده فى الدولاب.	fi baTaTeen/ makhaddaet ziyaeda fil doolaeb	There are spare blankets/pillows in the cupboard.
حط الزبالة... فى صندوق الزبالة	HoT izibaela... fi Sandoo' izzibaela	Put the rubbish... in the dustbin
فى الشارع	fishshari*	on the street
بيلموا الزبالة يوم...	biylemoo izzibaela yowm...	The rubbish is collected on...
عامل النظافة بيجى يوم...	*amil in naDaafa biyeegi yowm...	The cleaner comes on...
رقم موبيلى...	raqam mowbaili...	My mobile number is...
اعطى المفتاح... لى للجيران	a*Ti il moftaeH... li lilgeeraen	Give the key to... me the neighbour

food&drink

making bookings	89
at the restaurant	91
ordering your food	92
ordering your drinks	95
bars and cafés	97
comments and requests	99
special requirements	100
problems and complaints	102
paying the bill	102
buying food	103
menu reader	106

● There is a wide variety of food on offer throughout Arab countries. Some staples are 'Arabic bread' (*ªaysh baladi*) – flat and made from wheat dough; 'foreign' or French bread (*ªaysh fino*) and Lebanese bread (*ªaysh shaemi*), a type of thin pitta bread. Popular snack foods include stewed brown beans (*fool*), stuffed peppers or aubergines (*maHshi*) and deep fried bean balls (*felaefel* or *TaªmaYa*).

YOU MAY SEE...

البار الخارجى	*il **bar** il **khae**regi*	outdoor bar
التراس	*itteras*	terrace/outdoor seating area
التواليت	*ittwalit*	toilets
الحانة	*il **Hae**na*	inn/pub
الحمام	*il Hamaem*	cloakroom/ bathroom
الشواية	*ishsha**wa**ya*	barbecue/grill
الكافيتريا	*il kafe**ter**ya*	coffee bar
المطعم	*il maTªam*	restaurant
اخدم نفسك	*ikhdim **naf**sak*	self-service
بار	*bar*	bar
حجرة الطعام	*Hogrit iTTaªam*	dining room
حلويات شامية	*Halawiyaet shaemaya*	Lebanese and Syrian sweets
فراخ تيك اواى	*firaekh taekaway*	roast chicken takeaway
قهوة	*'ahwa*	café
كباب	*kabaeb*	charcoal-grilled lamb

كشك	*koshk*	kiosk
مأكولات تيك أواي	*ma'koolaet taekaway*	take away food
محل آلآيس كريم	*maHal il aiskreem*	ice-cream parlour
محل سندوتشات	*maHal sandwitshaet*	sandwich bar
محل عصير فواكة	*maHal ªaSeer fawaekih*	juice bar
مشروبات كحولية و مشروبات خفيفة	*mashroobaet koHolaya wi mashroobaet khafeefa*	alcoholic and soft drinks
مطعم اسماك	*maTªam asmaek*	seafood restaurant
مطعم الهامبورجر	*maTªam ilhamborgar*	burger bar
مطعم فول و فلافل	*maTªam fool wi felaefil*	felafel and beans (*fool*) bar
مطعم كشرى	*maTªam koshari*	koshari restaurant
مطعم وجبات سريعة	*maTªam wagabaet sariªa*	snack bar

✳ making bookings
(see **time phrases**, page 21)

● Lunch is eaten around 2-3pm, and is usually the main meal of the day. The evening meal is served from around 6pm till late in the evening.

YOU MAY WANT TO SAY...

My name is...	...اسمى	*ismi...*
My telephone/ mobile number is...	...رقم تليفونى/الموبايل هو	*raqam tilifowni/ mowbaili howa...*

food and drink

89

● I'd like to reserve a table for...
عايز/عايزة أحجز ترابيزة لـ...
ayiz (m)/*ayza* (f) aHgiz tarabayza lil...

two people
شخصين
shakhSayn

tomorrow evening at half past eight
بكرة الساعة الثامنة والنصف مساء
bokra issa*a tamanya wi noS mesa'

this evening at nine o'clock
الليلة الساعة التاسعة مساء
il ayla issa*a tes*a mesa'

● Could you get us a table...
ممكن حجز الترابيزة فى وقت...
momkin aHgiz il tarabayza fi wa't...

earlier?
بدري عن كده؟
badri *an keda

later?
متأخر عن كدة؟
met'akhar *an keda

حا تحجز الترابيزة الساعة كام؟	HateHgiz ittarabayza issa*a kaem	What time would you like the table for?
كام شخص؟	kaem shakhS	For how many people?
اسمك إيه؟	ismak ay	What's your name?
رقم التليفون من فضلك	raqam ittilifown min faDlak	What's your telephone number?
اسف المطعم كامل الحجز.	aesif/asfa il maT*am kaemil il Hagz	I'm sorry, we're fully booked.

food and drink

90

✳ at the restaurant

YOU MAY WANT TO SAY... 💬

●	I've booked a table.	انا حجزت ترابيزة.	*ana Hagazt tarabayza*
●	My name is...	أسمى...	*ismi...*
●	We haven't booked.	ما حجزناش ترابيزة.	*ma Hagaznaesh tarabayza*
●	Have you got a table for four, please?	عندك ترابيزة لأربعة أشخاص من فضلك؟	*ªandak (to m)/ªandik (to f) tarabayza li arbaªat ashkhaaS min faDlak (to m)/ faDlik (to f)*
●	Outside, if possible.	ممكن ترابيزة فى الخارج؟	*momkin tarabayza fil khaerig*
●	Have you got a high chair?	عندك كرسى عال للأطفال؟	*ªandak (to m)/ ªandik (to f) korsi ªaeli lil aTfaal*
●	How long's the wait?	كم مدة الأنتظار؟	*kaem mowdit il intiZar*
●	Can we wait at the bar?	ممكن ننتظر فى البار؟	*momkin nanTaZir fil bar*
●	Do you take credit cards?	بتقبلوا بطاقات الائتمان؟	*bite'balow biTa'aat li'timaen*

YOU MAY HEAR...

حجزتم؟	Hagaztom	Have you got a reservation?
تحبوا تقعدوا فين؟	teHeboo to'a°odoo fayn	Where would you like to sit?
مكان مخصص للتدخين اوعدم التدخين؟	makaen mokhaSaS liltadkheen aw °adam ittadkheen	Smoking or non-smoking?
لحظة واحدة من فضلك.	laHZa waHda min faDlak	Just a moment, please.
هل يمكنك الأنتظار؟	hael yomkinak il intiZar	Would you like to wait?
أسف المطعم... كامل العدد مغلق	asfa il maT°am... kaemil il °adad moghlaq	I'm sorry, we're... full closed
لا نقبل كروت الائتمان.	la na'bal koroot il i'timaen	We don't accept credit cards.

* ordering your food

● A variety of appetizers will usually be served before the main meal. Called mezza, these are small plates of mixed hors d'oeuvres: meats, vegetables, pickles, dips etc.

food and drink

YOU MAY WANT TO SAY...

- Excuse me! — عن أذنك! — *an iznak* (to m)/ *iznik* (to f)

- The menu, please. — المنيو من فضلك؟ — il *menyoo* min *faDlak* (to m)/*faDlik* (to f)

- Do you have... — عندك... — *andak* (to m)/*andik* (to f)...

  a children's menu? — قائمة طعام للأطفال؟ — *menyoo* Ta*am lil aTfaal

  vegetarian food? — قائمة طعام نباتي؟ — *menyoo* Ta*am nabaeti

  a set menu? — قائمة أطباق اليوم؟ — *menyoo* Ta*am il yowm

- Is it self-service? — أخدم نفسي؟ — akhdim nafsi

- We're ready to order. — نحن على استعداد للطلب. — eHna *ala iste*daed lilTalab

- Can I have...? — ممكن...؟ — momkin...

- I'd like... — عايز/عايزة... — *ayiz (m)/*ayza (f)...

  for starters — للمقدمات — lilmoqadimaet

  for the main course — للطبق الرئيسي — liTTaba' ir ra'eesi

  for dessert — للحلويات — lilHalawiyaet

- I'd like ... followed by... — عايز/عايزة ... و بعد كده... — *ayiz (m)/*ayza (f) ... wi ba*d keda...

- Does that come with vegetables? — الطبق ده مع الخضار؟ — iTTaba' da ma*a il khoDar

- What's this please? — إيه ده من فضلك؟ — ay da min faDlak (to m)/ faDlik (to f)

ordering your food

● What are today's specials?	ما هى وجبة اليوم؟	*ma haya wagbit il yowm*
● What's the local speciality?	ما هى أكلتكم المحلية المفضلة؟	*ma haya aklitkom ilmaHalaya ilmofaDalla*
● I'll have the same as him/her/them.	أنا عايز/عايزة زية/زيها/زيهم	*ana ªayiz (m)/ªayza (f) zayoo/zayaha/zayohom*
● I'd like it..., please.	عايزها مطبوخة....، من فضلك.	*ªayiz-ha (m) maTbookha..., min faDlak (to m)*
rare	على الريحة	*ªala ireeHa*
medium	نص نص	*noS noS*
well done	مستوية	*mistewaya*

تحبوا مشروب فى الأول؟	*teHeboo mashroob fil awil*	Would you like a drink first?
جاهزين للطلب؟	*gahzeen liT Talab*	Are you ready to order?
تحبوا إيه؟	*teHeboo ay...*	What would you like for...
ألمقبلات؟	*il moqabilaet*	starters?
الطبق الرئيسى؟	*iTTaba' irra'eesi*	the main course?
الحلويات؟	*il Halawiyaet*	dessert?
أحنا بنقترح...	*eHna binaqtareH...*	We recommend...
أسف الصنف ده خلص.	*aesif iSSanf da kheliS*	I'm sorry, that's finished.

food and drink

خدمة تانية؟	*khedma tanya*	**Anything else?**
إنه طريقة طهى تفضل؟	*ay Taree'it Tahi tefaDal*	**How would you like it cooked?**
تحب...	*teHeb...*	**Would you like...**
تشوف قائمة الحلويات؟	*tishoof qa'imat il Halawiyaet*	**to see the dessert menu?**
فنجال قهوة؟	*fingael 'ahwa*	**some coffee?**
بالهنا و الشفا!	*bilhana wi shefa*	**Enjoy your meal!**

✱ ordering your drinks

● Alcohol is not usually available in shops in Muslim countries. Attitudes towards alcohol do vary considerably: in Saudi Arabia, the sale or public consumption of alcohol is severely punished; in other countries, such as Egypt, Morocco and Jordan - where there are sizeable populations of non-Muslims - you can drink in some bars and restaurants. In most Middle Eastern countries you'll find alcohol in top-end hotels, nightclubs and duty-free shops.

YOU MAY WANT TO SAY...

● Can we see the wine list, please?

عايز قائمة النبيت من فضلك.

ᵃayiz (m)/*ᵃayza* (f) *qa'imit innebeet min faDlak* (to m)/ *faDlik* (to f)

● A bottle of this please.

زجاجة من النوع ده من فضلك.

zoogaega min inowᵃ da min faDlak (to m)/*faDlik* (to f)

food and drink

95

Half a litre of this please.	نصف لتر من النوع ده من فضلك.	noS litr min da min **faDlak** (to m)/ **faDlik** (to f)
A glass of this one, please.	كاس من النوع ده من فضلك.	kaes min **inow**ª da min **faDlak** (to m)/ **faDlik** (to f)
We'll have red/white wine, please.	حا نطلب نبيت (احمر/ أبيض) من فضلك.	Hano**Tlob** ne**beet** a**H**mar/a**byaD** min **faDlak** (to m)/ **faDlik** (to f)
What beers do you have?	إيه أنواع البيرة عندكم؟	ay anwaª il **bee**ra ª**andokom**
What wines do you have?	إيه أنواع النبيت عندكم؟	ay anwaª inne**beet** ª**andokom**
Is there a local wine?	عندكم نبيت محلى؟	ª**andokom** ne**beet** ma**Hali**
Can I have...	من فضلك ممكن...	min **faDlak** (to m)/ **faDlik** (to f) **momkin**...
a gin and tonic?	كاس جن مع التونيك؟	kaes jin **maªa** it**to**nik
a whisky?	كاس ويسكى؟	kaes **wis**ki
a vodka and coke?	كأس فودكا مع الكوكاكولا؟	kaes **vowd**ka **maªa** il **kow**ka **kow**la
A bottle of mineral water, please.	زجاجة مياة معدنية من فضلك؟	zoo**gae**git **mai**ya maª**da**naya min **faDlak** (to m)/ **faDlik** (to f)
What soft drinks do you have?	إيه المشروبات الخفيفة عندكم؟	ay il mashroo**baet** il kha**fee**fa ª**andokom**

bars and cafés

YOU MAY HEAR...

عايز لتر او نصف لتر؟	^a**ayiz** litr aw **noS** litr	Do you want a litre or a half litre?
عايز ثلج و ليمون؟	^a**ayiz** talg wi la**moon**	Ice and lemon?
عايز زجاجة مياة ايضآ؟	^a**ayiz** zoo**gae**git **mai**ya ka**maan**	Would you like water as well?
مياة فوارأو مياة طبيعية؟	**mai**ya fa**waar** aw **mai**ya Tabi^a**ey**ya	Sparkling or still water?
زجاجة كبيرة او زجاجة صغيرة؟	zoo**gae**ga ki**bee**ra aw zoo**gae**ga Sog**hai**yara	A large or small bottle?

✳ bars and cafés

● Tea and coffee are drunk extensively in the Middle East. Tea (*shay*) is served very sweet, either plain or with mint (*bilne^anae^a*), milk (*bilaban*), or with roots and spices such as ginger, caraway or cinnamon. If you want it without sugar, ask for *shay saeda*. English-style tea may be found in bigger hotels and restaurants. Thick black Turkish coffee is served in small cups. It will come extremely sweet unless you request 'without sugar' ('*ahwa saeda*), 'with very little sugar' ('*ahwa ^aalal reeHa*) or 'medium sweet' ('*ahwa mazbooT*). Instant coffee (*neskafay*) is also available, but is not as popular.

food and drink

97

YOU MAY WANT TO SAY...

I'll have ... please.	عايز/عايزة ... من فضلك	*a*yiz (m)/*a*yza (f) ... min faDlak (to m)/faDlik (to f)
a coffee	فنجان قهوة	fingael 'ahwa
a white coffee	قهوة باللبن	'ahwa bil laban
a black coffee	قهوة بدون لبن	'ahwa bidoon laban
a cup of tea	فنجان شاى	fingael shay
a fruit/herbal tea	فنجان شاى فواكه/أعشاب	fingael shay fawaekih/ *aa*shaeb
with milk/lemon	باللبن/بالليمون	bil laban/bil laemoon
with sugar	بالسكر	bissokkar
sweetner	سكر صناعى	sokkar Sina*a*i
A glass of...	كوباية...	kobbayit...
tap water	مياة طبيعية	maiya Tabee*a*aya
wine	نبيذ	nebeet
apple juice	عصير تفاح	*a*Seer tofaeH
No ice, thanks.	بدون ثلج شكراً.	bidoon talg shokran
Is this juice made with bottled water or tap water?	العصير ده معمول بمياة معدنية ولا بمياة من الحنفية؟	il *a*Seer da ma*a*mool bi maiya ma*a*danaya walla bi maiya min il Hanafaya
A bottle of water, please.	زجاجة مياة من فضلك.	zoogaegit maiya min faDlak (to m)/faDlik (to f)
A piece of...	قطعة من...	qeT*a*a min...
How much is that?	بكم ده؟	bikaem da

food and drink

98

YOU MAY HEAR...

اجيب لك إيه؟	*agiblak ay*	What can I get you?
تحب إيه؟	*teHib ay*	What would you like?
كبيرة او صغيرة؟	*kibeera aw Soghaiyara*	Large or small?
مياة طبيعية او فوار؟	*maiya Tabiªaya aw fawaar*	Still or fizzy?
بالثلج او بدون ثلج؟	*bil talg aw bidoon talg*	With or without ice?
فوراً.	*fawran*	Right away.
فاتورة واحدة او فاتورتين؟	*fatoora waHda aw fatoortayn*	Are you paying together or separately?

✳ comments and requests

YOU MAY WANT TO SAY...

- This is delicious! — ده لذيذ! — *da lazeez*
- Can I/we have more... — ممكن نطلب كمان ... من فضلك؟ — *momkin noTlob kamaen ... min faDlak* (to m)/*faDlik* (to f)

  bread, please? — عيش — *ªaysh*
  water, please? — مياة — *maiya*

- Can I/we have ... please? — ممكن نطلب ... من فضلك؟ — *momkin noTlob ... min faDlak* (to m)/*faDlik* (to f)

another bottle of wine	زجاجة نبيذ كمان	*zoogaegit nebeet kamaen*
another glass	كوبايا كمان	*kobbaya kamaen*
● I can't eat another thing.	مش ممكن أكل أى حاجة تانيه.	*mish momkin aekol ay Haga tanya*

YOU MAY HEAR...

| هل كل شيء على ما يرام؟ | *hael kol shai' ªala mai yoraam* | Is everything all right? |
| هل استمتعتم بالوجبة؟ | *hael istamtaªtom bil wagba* | Did you enjoy your meal? |

✳ special requirements

● Vegetarians will find they're well catered for in the Middle East, as meat-free dishes are part of the regular diet.

YOU MAY WANT TO SAY...

● I'm diabetic.	عندى مرض السكر.	*ªandi maraD issokkar*
● I'm allergic to...	عندى حساسية ضد...	*ªandi Hasasaya Ded...*
nuts	المكسرات	*il mikassaraat*
cow's milk	لبن البقر	*laban il ba'ar*
shellfish	لحم القواقع	*laHm il qawaaqeª*
● I'm vegetarian.	أنا نباتى.	*ana nebaeti*

food and drink

I don't eat meat or fish.	لا أكل اللحم او الأسماك.	*la aekol ilaHm aw il asmaek*
I don't eat any animal product.	لا أكل منتجات لحوم الحيوانات.	*la aekol montagaet loHoom il Haiwanaet*
I can't eat...	لا أستطيع اكل...	*la astaTeeª aekol...*
dairy products	منتجات الألبان	*montagaet il albaen*
wheat products	منتجات الشعير	*montagaet il sheªeer*
Do you have ... food?	هل عندك...؟	*hael ªandak (to m)/ ªandik (to f)...*
halal	لحم حلال	*laHm Halael*
free-range	لحم حيوانات طليقة	*laHm Haiwanaet Taleeqa*
low sodium	ملح قليل	*malH qaleel*
low fat	قليل الدسم	*qaleel iddasam*
Do you have anything without...	هل عندكم اى أكل بدون...	*hael ªandak (to m)/ªandik (to f) akl bidoon...*
meat?	لحم؟	*laHm*
Is that cooked with...	هل تم طبخ هذا...	*hael tam Tabkh haeza...*
butter?	بالزبد؟	*bizzebda*
garlic?	بالثوم؟	*bittowm*
Does that have ... in it?	هل هذا الأكل يحتوى على...؟	*hael haeza il akl yaHtawi ªala...*
nuts	مكسرات	*mikassaraat*

حأسال الطباخ.	Has'al iTTabakh	I'll check with the kitchen.
الأكل يحتوي على...	il akl yaHtawi ªala...	It's all got ... in it.
مكسرات	mikassaraat	nuts

* problems and complaints

- Excuse me.

  عن أذنك.   ªan iznak (to m)/
  iznik (to f)

- This is...

  هذا الأكل...   haeza il akl...
  - cold   بارد   baerid
  - underdone   غير مطبوخ جيداً   ghayr maTbookh gayedan
  - burnt   محروق   maHroo'

- I didn't order this.   لم أطلب هذا.   lam aTlob haeza

- I ordered the...   أنا طلبت...   ana Talabt...

- Is our food coming soon?

  من فضلك الأكل المطلوب   min faDlak (to m)/
  حا يجهز أمتى؟   faDlik (to f) il akl
  il maTloob
  Haiyighaz emta

* paying the bill

- The bill, please.   الحساب من فضلك.   il Hisaeb min faDlak (to m)/
  faDlik (to f)

food and drink

● Is service included?	هل الحساب يشمل الخدمة؟	hael il Hisaeb yeshmal il khedma
● There's a mistake on the bill.	فى خطأ فى الحساب.	fi khaTa' fil Hisaeb
● That was fantastic, thank you.	ممتاز شكرا.	momtaez shokran

* buying food

YOU MAY WANT TO SAY... 💬

● I'd like ... please.	عايز/عايزة ... من فضلك.	ªayiz (m)/ªayza (f) ... min faDlak (to m)/faDlik (to f)
some of those/ that	شوية من ده	showaiya min da
half a kilo (of ...)	نصف كيلو...	noS keeloo...
two hundred grammes of that	ماتان جرام من ده	mitayn gram min da
a piece of that	قطعة من ده	qeTªa min da
two slices of that	شريحتين من ده	shariHatayn min da

How much is...	...بكام	*bikaem...*
that?	ده	*da*
a kilo of cheese?	كيلو الجبن؟	*keeloo il gebna*
What's that, please?	إيه ده من فضلك	*ay da min faDlak* (to m)/*faDlik* (to f)
Have you got...	هل عندك...	*hael ªandak* (to m)/*ªandik* (to f)...
any bread?	خبز؟	*khobz*
any more?	كمان شوية؟	*kamaen showaiya*
A bit more/less please.	اكتر شوية/أقل شوية من فضلك.	*aktar showaiya/aqal showaiya min faDlak* (to m)/*faDlik* (to f)
That's enough, thank you.	كفاية شكراً.	*kifaya shokran*
I'm looking for the ... section.	انا ابحث عن قسم...	*ana abHas ªan qesm...*
dairy	منتجات الألبان	*montagaet il albaen*
fruit and vegetable	الفواكة والخضروات	*il fawaekih wil khoDrawaat*
Can I have a bag please?	ممكن كيس من فضلك؟	*momkin kees min faDlak* (to m)/*faDlik* (to f)

YOU MAY HEAR...

هل تحتاج مساعدة؟	hael **meH**taeg mosaªda	Can I help you?
تحب إيه؟	te**Heb**/te**Heb**i ay	What would you like?
عابز قد إيه؟	ªa**yiz** 'ad ay	How much would you like?
عايزة كام قطعة؟	ª**ay**za kaem qeTªa	How many would you like?
أسف الصنف ده خلص.	**ae**sif iSSanf da khe**liS**	I'm sorry, we've sold out.
اى خدمة ثانية؟	ay **khed**ma	Anything else?

menu reader

GENERAL

اطباق اليوم	aTbaa' il yowm	set dishes
الا كارت	ala kart	à la carte menu
الأطباق التقليدية	il aTbaq ittaqlidaya	typical dishes
الأفطار	il ifTar	breakfast
الحساب (لا) يشمل الخدمة	il Hisaeb (la) yashmal il khedma	service (not) included
الحساب يشمل الضريبة	il Hisaeb yashmal il Dareeba	tax included
العشاء	il ªasha	dinner
الغذاء	il ghada	lunch
أبراتيف	apereteef	aperitifs
أكلات خفيفة	akalaet khafeefa	snacks
طبق اليوم	Taba' il yowm	dish of the day
طبيخ بيتى	Tabeekh bayti	home cooking
محلى	maHali	local
نحن (لا) نقبل بطاقات الأتمان	naHnoo (la) naqbal biTaqaat il i'timaen	We (do not) accept credit cards
وجبات اليوم	wagabaet il yowm	set menu
وجبات للسياح	wagabaet lilsoiyaeH	tourist menu

CLASSIC DISHES

شوربة عدس	shorbit ªats	lentil soup
شاورمة	shawerma	spit-roasted meat, thinly sliced
طعمية	Taªmaya	deep fried chickpea burgers

فلافل	*falaefil*	deep fried chick pea burgers
فاصوليا بصلصة الطماطم	*fasolya biSalSit iTTamaTim*	beans in tomato sauce
فول	*fool*	stewed dried beans
كباب	*kabaeb*	shish kebab
كبيبة	*kobaeba*	deep fried balls of mincemeat and cracked wheat
كشرى	*koshari*	lentils, rice and pasta
كفتة	*kofta*	meatballs
ملوخية	*molokhaya*	green leaf cooked in stock
ورق عنب	*wara' ᵃenab*	stuffed vine leaves

WAYS OF COOKING

بالبخار	*bil bokhaar*	steamed
بالبخار/فى الفرن	*bil bookhar/fil forn*	braised
صوص الباشاميل	*SowS il beshamel*	béchamel sauce
صوص الخل	*SowS il khal*	vinaigrette
فى الفرن	*fil forn*	roast
متبل	*mitabil*	marinated
محشى	*maHshi*	stuffed
محمر	*maHammar*	fried
مخبوز	*makhbooz*	baked
مخلل	*mikhalil*	pickled, marinated
مدخن	*midakhan*	smoked
مسلوق	*masloo'*	boiled, stewed
مشوى	*mashwi*	barbecued, grilled

food and drink

107

MEAT

أرنب	*arnab*	rabbit
بسطرمة	*basTerma*	pastourma (garlic-cured beef)
بط	*baTa*	duck
بقرى	*baqari*	beef
حمامة	*Hamaema*	pigeon
سجق	*sogoq*	sausage
سجق بالبهارات	*sogoq bilboharaat*	spicy sausage
سكالوب	*iskalob*	escalop
ضلع	*Delaᵃ*	ribs
ديك رومى	*deek roomi*	turkey
فراخ	*firaekh*	chicken
كلاوى	*kalaewi*	kidneys
كبدة	*kebda*	liver
كرشة	*kirsha*	tripe
لحم بفتيك	*laHm boftaek*	steak
لحم بقرى	*laHm baqari*	beef
لحم خنزير	*laHm khanzeer*	ham
لحم خنزير	*laHm khanzeer*	pork
لحم ضانى	*laHm Daani*	lamb
لحم غزال	*laHm ghazael*	venison
لحم فيلية	*laHm filay*	fillet steak
لحم كاندوز	*laHm kandooz*	veal
لحم معيز صغير	*laHm maᵃez Soghaiyar*	kid
لحم مفروم	*laHm mafroom*	minced meat
لحوم باردة	*loHowm barda*	cold meats
ماعز	*maᵃez*	goat

FISH

أخطبوط	*akhTabooT*	octopus
بطارخ	*baTaarekh*	fish eggs
بلح البحر	*balaH il baHr*	mussels
تونة	*toona*	tuna
جنبري	*ganbari*	prawns
جنبري	*ganbari*	shrimps
جنبري كبير	*ganbari kibeer*	king prawn
جندوفلى	*gandofli*	oysters
سردين	*sardeen*	sardines
سلمون (مدخن)	*salamown (midakhan)*	salmon (smoked)
سمك الأنشوجة	*samak il anshooga*	anchovies
سمك الثعابين	*samak it taªabeen*	eel
سمك ماكريل	*samak makril*	mackerel
سمك محمر مشكل	*samak maHammar mishakkil*	mixed fried fish
سمك مرجان	*samak morgaen*	red mullet
سمك موسى	*samak moussa*	sole
سمك وقار	*samak w'aar*	sea bass
كابوريا	*kaboriya*	crab
كيركند	*kerkind*	lobster

GENERAL FOOD

رز	*roz*	rice
اعشاب	*aªshaeb*	herbs
اعشاب مشكلة	*aªshaeb mishakkila*	mixed herbs
بقدونس	*ba'doonis*	parsley
ريحان	*riHaen*	basil

زعتر	za^atar	thyme
كزبرة خضراء	kozbara khaDra'	fresh coriander
نعناع	ne^anae^a	mint
بقول	boqool	pulses
حمص	HomoS	chickpeas
عدس	^aats	lentils
فاصوليا	fasolya	beans
بهارات	boharaat	spices
جوزة الطيب	gozt iTTeeb	nutmeg
حبهان	Habahaen	cardamom
شطة	shaTTa	chilli
قرفة	qerfa	cinnamon
قرنفل	qoronfil	clove
كزبرة	kozbara	coriander
كمون	kamoon	cumin
بون بون	bonbon	sweets
بيض	bayD	eggs
اوملیت	owmlet	omelette
بيض مسلوق	bayD masloo'	hard boiled
بيض مقلى	bayD maqli	fried
خضار	khoDar	vegetables
اسباراجاس	isbaragas	asparagus
أفوكادو	avokado	avocado
بازنجان	bitingaen	aubergine
بامية	bamya	okra
بسلة	bissella	peas
بصل	baSal	onion
بطاطس	baTaaTis	potatoes
بنجر	bangar	beetroot
ثوم	towm	garlic
جزر	gazar	carrot
خرشوف	kharshoof	artichokes
خس	khas	lettuce

خضار محشى	kho**Dar** ma**H**shi	stuffed vegetables
خضار مشكل	kho**Dar** mishak**kil**	mixed vegetables
خيار	**khey**aar	cucumber
خيار مخلل	**khey**aar mekha**l**il	gherkin
راس الفجل	ras il **figl**	radish
زرة	zo**ra**	sweetcorn
زيتون	zay**toon**	olives
سبانخ	sabae**nikh**	spinach
سلاطة	sala**Ta**	salad
طماطم	Tama**Tim**	tomato
فاصوليا	fa**sol**ya	beans
فول أخضر	fool **akh**Dar	green beans
قرنبيط	qarna**beeT**	cauliflower
كرات	ko**raat**	leek
كرفس	ka**rafs**	celery
كرنب	ko**ronb**	cabbage
كرنب أحمر	ko**ronb a**Hmar	red cabbage
كوسة	**kow**sa	courgette
كوسة	**kow**sa	marrow
ماشروم	mush**room**	mushroom
طرشى	**Tor**shi	pickled vegetables

خل	khal	vinegar
زيت الزيتون	zayt zay**toon**	olive oil
سكر	**sok**kar	sugar
سكر صناعى	**sok**kar Sina³i	sweetener
سمسم	**sim**sim	sesame seed
سندوتش	**sand**witch	sandwich
شوربة	**shor**ba	soup
شوربة عدس	**shor**bit ³ats	lentil soup
شوربة كونسومية	**shor**ba konsow**may**	clear soup

شوكولاتة	shokolaata	chocolate
صوص	SowS	sauce
عسل	ªasal	honey
عيش	ªaysh	bread
عيش بالحبوب	ªaysh bil Hoboob	granary/wholemeal bread
عيش بلدى	ªaysh baladi	Arabic bread
عيش شامى	ªaysh shaemi	Lebanese bread
عيش فينو	ªaysh fino	French bread
عيش فينو صغير	ªaysh fino Soghaiyar	bread roll
توست	towst	toast
فاكهة	fakha	fruit
أراسيا	arasya	prune
أناناس	ananaes	pineapple
برتقال	borto'aen	orange
برقوق	barqooq	plum
بطيخ	baTeekh	watermelon
بلح	balaH	date
تفاح	tifaeH	apple
تين	teen	fig
جوافة	gwaefa	guava
جوز الهند	gowz il hind	coconut
خوخ	khokh	peach
زبيب	zibeeb	raisins
رمان	rommaan	pomegranate
شمام	shamaem	cantaloupe melon
عنب	ªenab	grapes
فراولة	farawla	strawberry
كريز	kerez	cherry
كمثرى	kommetra	pear
ليمون	laemoon	lemon

مانجة	*man*ga	mangoe
مشمش	*mish*mish	apricot
موز	*mowz*	banana
يوسف أفندى	*yoosta*fendi	tangerines
فانيلا	*vani*lya	vanilla
فلفل	*fil*fil	pepper
فلفل أحمر	*fil*fil aHmar	red
فلفل أخضر	*fil*fil akhDar	green
فلفل حار	*fil*fil Har	hot
كسكسى	*koos*koosi	couscous
لب	*leb*	watermelon seeds
مكسرات	*mikassa*raat	nuts
البندق	*il bon*do'	almonds
عين جمل	ªayn *ga*mal	walnuts
فول سودانى	*fool soo*daeni	peanuts
مايونيز	*maiyow*nayz	mayonnaise
مربى	*me*rabba	jam
جبن	*geb*na	cheese
جبنة بيضاء	*geb*na bayDa	white
جبنة رومى	*geb*na roomi	hard
جبنة قريش	*geb*na qaereesh	thick creamy
جبنة مالحة	*geb*na malHa	salted curd
جبنة بلبن المعيز	*geb*na min *la*ban il maªez	goat's milk cheese
لبنة	*lab*na	curd
مش	*mish*	mature
زبادى	*ze*baedi	yoghurt
زبدة	*zeb*da	butter
كريم	*kray*ma	cream
لبن	*la*ban	milk
مارجرين	*marja*reen	margarine
مستردة	*mos*tarda	mustard
مكرونة	*maka*rowna	pasta

شعرية	*she*ª*raya*	noodles
مكرونة سباجيتى	*maka***row***na* *spa***get***ti*	spaghetti
ملح	*malH*	salt
موسمى	*maow***se***mi*	seasonal
مياة الورد	*mai*yit *il ward*	rosewater

DESSERTS

أم على	*om* ª*ali*	raisin cake with warm milk
ايس كريم	*ais***kreem**	ice-cream
بسبوسة	*bas***boo***sa*	semolina cake
بقلاوة	*baq***lae***wa*	filo pastry with nuts and honey (baklava)
بليلة	*bi***lee***la*	nuts, raisins, wheat and milk
زلابية	*zala***baya***	pastries dipped in rosewater
سوربية	*sor***bay**	sorbet
قطايف	*qa***Tai***yif*	pastry filled with nuts
كاسترد	*kas*tard	egg custard
كنافة	*ko***nae***fa*	shredded pastry with nuts and honey
كيكة	*kay*ka	(sponge) cake
ملبن	*mal*ban	turkish delight
مهلبية	*mahala***baya***	rice or cornflour pudding

DRINKS

براندى	*brandi*	brandy
بيرة	*beera*	beer
بيرة بدون كحول	*beera bidoon koHol*	alcohol-free
بيرة فى زجاجة	*beera fi zoogaega*	bottled
بيرة محلية	*beera maHalaya*	local
بيرة مستوردة	*beera mostawrada*	imported
تونيك	*tonik*	tonic
ثلج	*talg*	ice
حلو	*Helew*	sweet
روم	*room*	rum
زجاجة	*zoogaega*	bottle
صودا	*sowda*	soda
شاى	*shay*	tea
شاى أعشاب	*shay aªshaeb*	herbal tea
شاى بالليمون	*shay bilaemoon*	tea with lemon
شاى بالنعناع	*shay binneªnaeª*	mint tea
شاى باللبن	*shay bilaban*	tea with milk
شاى مثلج	*shay mothalag*	iced tea
قرفة	*qerfa*	cinnamon tea
شمبانيا	*shambanya*	champagne
شيح بابونى	*sheeH babooni*	camomile tea
عصير	*ªaSeer*	juice
عصير الأناناس	*ªaSeer il ananaes*	pineapple
عصير البرتقال	*ªaSeer il borto'aen*	orange
عصير التفاح	*ªaSeer ittifaeH*	apple
عصير التمر هندى	*ªaSeer ittamrHindi*	tamarind
عصير الجريب فروت	*ªaSeer il graybfroot*	grapefruit
عصير الرمان	*ªaSeer il rommaan*	pomegranate
عصير القصب	*ªaSeer il qaSab*	sugar cane

عصير الطماطم	ªaSeer iTTamaaTim	tomato
فودكا	vowdka	vodka
قهوة	'ahwa	coffee
قهوة امريكانى	'ahwa amrikaeni	American
قهوة بالفلتر	'ahwa bil filter	filter
قهوة باللبن	'ahwa bil laban	white
قهوة من غير كافيين	'ahwa min ghayr kafyeen	decaffeinated
قهوة من غير لبن	'ahwa min ghayr laban	black
قهوة تركى	'ahwa torki	Turkish coffee
قهوة زيادة	'ahwa ziyaeda	very sweet
قهوة سادة	'ahwa saeda	without sugar
قهوة مظبوط	'ahwa mazbooT	medium-sweet
قهوة مثلجة	'ahwa mothalaga	iced
كاكاو (سخن/مثلج)	kakaw (sokhn/ mothalag)	chocolate (hot/ cold)
كوكتيل	koktayl	cocktail
كونياك	konyaek	cognac
كوب	kobaya	glass
لبن (ساخن/بارد)	laban (sokhn/baerid)	milk (hot/cold)
ليمونادة	limonaeta	lemonade
مياة معدنية	maiya maªdanaya	mineral water
فوار	fawaar	sparkling
ميلك شايك	milk shayk	milkshake
نبيذ	nebeet	wine
نبيذ محلى	nebeet maHali	local wine
نبيذ أحمر	nebeet aHmar	red
نبيذ روز	nebeet rowz	rosé
نبيذ حلو	nebeet Helw	sweet
نبيذ أبيض	nebeet abyaD	white
ويسكى	wiski	whisky

at the tourist office   118
opening times   119
visiting places   120
going on tours and trips   124
tourist glossary   125
entertainment   126
booking tickets   128
at the show   129
sports and activities   130
at the beach, river or pool   133

sightseeing
&activities

✳ at the tourist office

YOU MAY SEE...

تذاكر	*tazaekir*	tickets
خرائط	*kharayiT*	maps
مغلق	*moghlaq*	closed
مفتوح	*maftooH*	open
هوتيلات	*hotelaet*	hotels

YOU MAY WANT TO SAY...

● Do you speak English?
بتتكلم/بتتكلمى انجليزى؟
bititkalim (to m)/ *bititkalimi* (to f) *ingleezi*

● Do you have...
عندك...
ªandak (to m)/ *ªandik* (to f)...

   a map of the town?
خريطة للمدينة؟
khareeTit il madeena

   a list of hotels?
لستة هوتيلات؟
listit hotelaet

● Can you recommend a...
ممكن تدلنا على...
momkin tidilena ªala...

   cheap hotel?
هوتيل رخيص؟
hotel rakheeS

   traditional restaurant?
مطعم شعبى؟
maTªam shaªbi

● Do you have information...
عندك معلومات...
ªandak (to m)/*ªandik* (to f) *maªloomaet...*

   in English?
بألأنجليزى؟
bilingleezi

   about opening times?
عن مواعيد العمل؟
ªan mowaªeed il ªamal

- Can you book... | ...ممكن تحجز لى | *momkin teHgizli...*
  - a hotel room for me? | غرفة فى الهوتيل؟ | *ghorfa fi il hotel*
  - this day trip for me? | مكان فى الرحلة دى؟ | *makaen fi irreHla di*
- Where is the... | ...فين | *fayn...*
  - bank? | البنك؟ | *il bank*
- Is there a post office near here? | فى مكتب بريد قريب من هنا؟ | *fi maktab bareed orayyib min hena*
- Can you show me on the map? | فين المكان على الخريطة؟ | *fayn il makaen ªala il khareeTa*

✳ opening times
(see **telling the time**, page 20)

YOU MAY WANT TO SAY...

- What time does the... open? | بيفتح... الساعة كام؟ | *...biyeftaH issaªa kaem*
  - museum | المتحف | *il matHaf*
- What time does the ... close? | بيقفل الساعة كام؟... | *...biye'fil issaªa kaem*
  - mosque | مسجد | *masgid*
- Is it open... | ...بيفتح | *biyeftaH...*
  - on Mondays? | يوم الأثنين؟ | *yowm il itnayn*
  - at the weekend? | فى الويكند؟ | *fi il weekend*
- Is it open to the public? | هل مفتوح للزوار؟ | *hael maftooH lizzoowar*

YOU MAY HEAR...

بيفتح كل يوم ما عدا...	biye**ftaH** kol **yowm** ma ªada...	It's open every day except...
مفتوح من... لحد...	maf**tooH** min... li**Had**...	It's open from... to...
مغلق يوم...	**mogh**laq **yowm**...	It's closed on...
مغلق فى الشتاء.	**mogh**laq fi is**sheta**	It's closed in winter.
مغلق للصيانة.	**mogh**laq li**SSiyaana**	It's closed for repairs.

* visiting places

● Dress code is important especially when visiting a mosque. Women should cover their hair, and avoid short, tight or revealing clothes. Remember to talk quietly once inside.

YOU MAY SEE...

خاص	**khaaS**	private
دورات بمصاحبة دليل	**daw**raat bimow**SaHabit** da**leel**	guided tours
مغلق (للترميم)	**mogh**laq (lil tar**meem**)	closed (for restoration)
مكتب التذاكر	**mak**tab itta**zaekir**	ticket office

ممنوع التصوير بالفلاش	*mamnoo^a ittaSweer bil flash*	no flash photography
ممنوع الدخول	*mamnoo^a iddokhool*	no entry
ممنوع اللمس	*mamnoo^a illams*	do not touch
مواعيد الدخول	*mawa^aeed iddokhool*	opening hours

YOU MAY WANT TO SAY...

- How much does it cost?

  بكام؟ *bikaem*

- One ticket, please.

  تذكرة من فضلك. *tazkara min faDlak* (to m)/*faDlik* (to f)

- Two adult tickets, please.

  تزكرتين من فضلك. *tazkartayn min faDlak* (to m)/*faDlik* (to f)

- One adult and two children, please.

  تذكرة كاملة و أثنين للأطفال من فضلك؟ *tazkara kamla wi itnayn lil aTfaal min faDlak* (to m)/*faDlik* (to f)

- A family ticket, please.

  تذكرة للعائلة. *tazkara lil ^aa'ila min faDlak* (to m)/*faDlik* (to f)

- Is there a discount for...

  فى تخفيض... *fi takhfeeD...*
  - students?

    للطلبة؟ *lil Talaba*
  - senior citizens?

    للمسنين؟ *lil mosineen*
  - children?

    للأطفال؟ *lil aTfaal*

● Is there...	...فى	fi...
wheelchair access?	مكان لكراسى المعوقين؟	makaen li karesi ilmoªawaqeen
an audio tour?	دورات صوتية بالسماعات؟	dawraat Sawtaya bissamªaet
● Are there guided tours (in English)?	فى دورات مع دليل باللغة الأنجليزية؟	fi dawraat maªa daleel bilogha ilingleezaya
● Can I take photos?	ممكن اخذ صور؟	momkin akhod Sowar
● Can you take a photo of us?	ممكن تاخذ لنا صورة؟	momkin taekhod lina Soora
● When was this built?	اتبنى امتى؟	itbana emta
● Who painted that?	من رسم ده؟	meen rasam da
● How old is it?	عمرة قد إيه؟	ªomro 'addi ay

YOU MAY HEAR...

ثمنة خمسة و عشرين حنية للفرد.	tamano khamsa wi ªishreen ginee lil fard	It costs L.E. 25 per person.
فى تخفيض...	fi takhfeeD...	There's a discount for...
للطلبة	liTTalaba	students

اولادك عندهم كام سنة؟	awlaedak ªandohom kaem sana	How old are your children?
الأطفال تحت سن ... مجاناً.	il aTfaal taHt sin ... magaenan	Children under ... go free.
المكان مجهز لكراسى المعوقين.	il makaen mogahaz li karaesi ilmoªawaqeen	There are wheelchair ramps.
أنا اسف المكان غير مناسب لكراسى المعوقين.	ana aesif il makaen ghayr monaesib li karaesi ilmoªawaqeen	I'm sorry, it's not suitable for wheelchairs.
عايزة تشتركي فى دورة؟	ªayza tishterki fi dawra	Do you want to join a tour?
الدورة الصوتية ثمنها...	iddawra iSSawtaya tamanha...	The audio tour costs...
الرسام/المعمارى كان...	irrasaem/il maªmaeri kaen...	The painter/ architect was...
اتبنى فى القرن ال...	itbana fi il qarn il...	It was built in the ... century.
اترسمت فى...	itrasamit fi...	It was painted in...
سنة الف و تسعمائة وأثنى عشرة سنة	sanat alf wi tosªomaya wi itnashar	1912
الثمانينات	il tamaneenaet	the eighties

123

* going on tours and trips

YOU MAY WANT TO SAY...

● We'd like to join the tour to...	احنا عايزين نشترك فى دورة...	*ehna ªayzeen nishterik fi dawra...*
● What time does it leave?	بتبداء الساعة كام؟	*bitebda' issaªa kaem*
● What time does it get back?	العودة الساعة كام؟	*il ªawda issaªa kaem*
● How long is it?	ألمدة قد إيه؟	*il modda 'addi ay*
● Where does it leave from?	بتبداء منين؟	*bitebda' minayn*
● Does the guide speak English?	الدليل بيتكلم انجليزى؟	*iddaleel biyetkalim ingleezi*
● How much is it?	بكام؟	*bikaem*
● Is ... included? lunch accommodation	شامل... الغداء السكن	*shaemil...* *il ghada* *issakan*
● When's the next trip?	الرحلة القادمة الساعة كام؟	*irreHla il qadema issaªa kaem*
● Can we hire... an English-speaking guide?	ممكن نأجر... دليل بيتكلم انجليزى؟	*momkin ni'agar...* *daleel biyetkalim ingleezi*
● I'd like to see...	أنا عايز اشوف/احنا عايزين نشوف...	*ana ªayiz (m)/ªayza (f) ashoof...*
● We'd like to see...	احنا عايزين نشوف...	*eHna ªayzeen nishoof...*

YOU MAY HEAR...

بيقوم الساعة...	biy'oom issaªa...	It leaves at...
بيرجع الساعة...	yergaª issaªa...	It gets back at...
بيقوم من...	biy'oom min...	It leaves from...
الرجاء عدم التأخير!	irragaª ªadam itta'kheer	Don't be late!
بيحاسب/بتحاسب باليوم	biyHaesib/ bitHaesib ... bil yowm	He/She charges ... per day.

* tourist glossary

YOU MAY SEE...

المدافن	il madaefin	cemetery
استاد	istaed	stadium
برج	borg	tower
حديقة	Hadeeqa	gardens
عين سخنة	ªayn sokhna	hot spring
قصر	qaSr	palace
قلعة	qalªa	castle
لوحة	lowHa	portrait
مسجد	masgid	mosque
معبد	maªbad	temple
معرض	maªraD	exhibition
معرض فنى	maªraD fanni	art gallery
ميدان	midaen	square
نصب تذكارى	naSb tizkaeri	monument
هدايا للذكرى	hadayya lil zekra	souvenirs

✱ entertainment

الصف	iSSaf	row
المدخل	il **mad**khal	entrance
اوركسترا	or**kes**tra	orchestra
ارض السباق	arD is**si**baq	racecourse
بالية	**bal**lay	ballet
حجرة الأمانات	**Hog**rit il ama**naet**	cloakroom
حفلة المساء	**Haf**lit il mae**sae'**	evening performance
خروج	kho**roog**	exit
دار الأوبرا	**dar** il **ob**ra	opera house
سرك	sirk	circus
سينما	si**ne**ma	cinema
كامل العدد	**kae**mil il ªadad	sold out
ماتش	mutch	match
ماتينية	mati**nay**	matinée
نادي ليلي	**nae**di **lay**li	nightclub
اللغة الأصلية مع الترجمة	il **lo**gha il aS**la**ya maªa it**tar**gama	original language version with subtitles
تذاكر حفل اليوم	ta**zae**kir Hafl il yowm	tickets for today's performance
فوق سن ثمانية عشرة سنة فقط	fow' sin taman**ta**shar **sa**na **fa**qaT	over 18s only
مفيش استراحة	ma**feesh** isti**ra**Ha	there is no interval
ممنوع الدخول بعد بداية العرض	mam**noo**ª id**do**khool baªd bi**da**yit il ªard	no entry once the performance has begun

YOU MAY WANT TO SAY...

Where can we go tonight?	حانروح فين الليلة؟	Hanroh fayn illayla
What's on...	إيه البرنامج...	ay il bernaemig...
tomorrow?	بكرة؟	bokra
at the theatre?	فى المسرح؟	fil masraH
at the cinema?	فى السينما؟	fissinema
Can we see...	ممكن نتفرج...	momkin nitfarag...
belly dancing?	رقص بلداى	ra'S baladi
Is there a football match on this weekend?	فى ماتش كورة فى الويكند؟	fi mutch kora fil weekend
When does the ... start?	متى يبدأ...	mata yebda'...
game	الماتش	il mutch
What time does it finish?	متى ينتهى؟	mata yentehi
How long is it?	لمدة قد إيه؟	limodit 'ad ay
Do we need to book?	لازم نحجز؟	laezim neHgiz
Where can I get tickets?	أشترى التذاكر منين؟	ashteri ittazaekir minayn
Is it suitable for children?	هل مناسب للأطفال؟	hael monaesib lil aTfaal
Has the film got subtitles?	هل الفيلم مترجم؟	hael il film motargam
Is it dubbed?	هل الفيلم مدبلج؟	hael il film modablag

sightseeing and activities

127

YOU MAY HEAR...

...بتبدأ الساعة	biyebda' issaªa...	It starts at...
...بتنتهى الساعة	biyentehi issaªa...	It finishes at...
...لمدة	limodit...	It lasts about...
ساعتين	saªtayn	two hours
.من الأفضل الحجز مقدماً	min il afDal il Hagz mo'adaman	It's best to book in advance.
.مترجم باللغة الأنجليزية	motargam bilogha ilingleezaya	It's got English subtitles.
.يمكن شراء تذاكر هنا	yomkin shira' tazaekir hena	You can buy tickets here.

✳ booking tickets

YOU MAY WANT TO SAY...

- Can you get me tickets for...
  ...ممكن اشترى تذاكر ل
  momkin ashteri tazaekir li...

  the ballet?
  البالية؟
  il ballay

  the theatre?
  المسرح؟
  il masraH

- Are there any seats left for Saturday?
  فى تذاكر لحفلة يوم السبت؟
  fi tazaekir li Haflit yowm issabt

- I'd like to book...
  ...أنا عايز احجز
  ana ªayiz (m)/ ªayza (f) aHgiz...

- Do you have anything cheaper?
  عندك تذاكر ارخص؟
  ªandak (to m)/ªandik (to f) tazaekir arkhaS

YOU MAY HEAR... ?

كام؟	kaem	How many?
لأمتى؟	li'emta	When for?
أنا اسف مفيش كراسى فى حفلة المتينى/الليلة.	ana aesif mafeesh karesi fi Haflit il matinay/ilayla	I'm sorry we're sold out that day/ night.

✳ at the show

YOU MAY WANT TO SAY...

● Two for tonight's performance, please.

تذكرتين لحفلة الليلة من فضلك؟

tazkartayn li Haflit ilayla min faDlak (to m)/faDlik (to f)

● How much is that?

بكام؟

bikaem

● We'd like to sit...
  at the front
  at the back
  in the middle

عايزين نقعد...
فى المقدمة
فى المؤخرة
فى الوسط

ayzeen no'^aod...
fi il moqadema
fi il mo'akhera
fi il wesT

● We've reserved seats.

احنا حاجزين.

eHna Hagzeen

● My name is...

انا اسمى...

ana ismi...

● Is there an interval?

فى الأستراحة؟

fi ilisteraHa

● Can you stop talking, please?!

كفاية كلام من فضلك

kifaya kalaem min faDlak (to m)/ faDlik (to f)

sightseeing and activities

129

YOU MAY HEAR...

اسف المكان كامل العدد الليلة.	aesif il makaen kaemil il ªadad illayla	Sorry, we're full tonight.
عايزة تقعدى فين؟	ªayza to'ªodi fayn	Where do you want to sit?
تحب نسخة من البروجرام؟	teHeb noskha min il brogram	Would you like a programme?

* sports and activites

YOU MAY SEE...

الشاطىء	ishshaaTi'	beach
اسعاف اولى	isªaef awali	first aid
حمام سباحة (خارجى)	Hamaem sibaHa (khaeregi)	swimming pool (outdoor)
حمام سباحة (داخلى)	Hamaem sibaHa (daekheli)	swimming pool (indoor)
خاص	khaaS	private property
خطر	khaTar	danger
ركوب الخيل	rokoob il khayl	horse riding
مركب للأيجار	markib lil iygar	boat hire
مركز رياضى	markaz riyaaDi	sports centre
ملعب الجولف	malªab golf	golf course
ملعب تنس	malªab tenis	tennis court
ملعب كرة قدم	malªab korit qadam	football pitch
ممنوع السباحة	mamnooª issibaHa	no swimming
ممنوع الصيد	mamnooª iSSayd	no fishing

YOU MAY WANT TO SAY...

Where can I/we play...	العب/نلعب ... فين؟	*al^aab/nel^aab ... fayn*
tennis?	تنس؟	*tenis*
golf?	جولف؟	*golf*
Can I/we...	ممكن...	*momkin...*
go riding?	اركب/نركب خيل؟	*arkab/nerkab khael*
go fishing?	استاد/نستاد سمك؟	*asTaad/nisTaad samak*
go swimming?	أعوم/نعوم؟	*a^aoom/na^aoom*
I'm...	انا...	*ana...*
a beginner	مبتدىء	*mobtadi'*
quite experienced	مستوى متقدم	*mostawa motaqadim*
How much does it cost...	بكام...	*bikaem...*
per hour?	فى الساعة؟	*fi issa^aa*
per day?	فى اليوم؟	*fi il yowm*
per week?	فى الأسبوع؟	*fi il izboo^a*
Can I/we hire...	ممكن نأجر...	*momkin n'aggar...*
clubs?	مضارب الجولف؟	*maDarib golf*
tennis rackets?	مضارب التنس؟	*maDarib tenis*
Do you give lessons?	فيه دروس خاصة؟	*fi doroos khaSa*
Do I/we have to be a member?	هل لابد أن أكون عضوآ؟	*hael labod an akoon ^aoDw*
Can children do it too?	هل مسموح أن يشترك الأطفال؟	*hael masmooH an yeshterik il aTfaal*

sightseeing and activities

131

- Is there a discount for children? | فية تخفيض للأطفال؟ | *fi takhfeeD lil aTfaal*
- Is the water warm? | هل المياة دافية؟ | *hael il maiya dafya*
- Is the water cold? | هل المياة باردة | *hael il maiya barda*

YOU MAY HEAR...

هل انت مبتدىء؟	*hael enta mobtadi'*	Are you a beginner?
هل تستطيع... التزحلق على المياة؟	*hael tastaTeeª...* *ittazaHloq ªala il maiya*	Can you... waterski?
الغوص؟	*il ghoS*	dive
ثمنه خمسين جنيه في الساعة.	*tamano khamseen ginee fissaªa*	It costs L.E. 50 per hour.
لازم تسيب عربون خمسة وعشرين جنية	*laezim teseeb ªarboon khamsa wi ªishreen ginee*	There's a refundable deposit of L.E. 25.
كامل العدد.	*kaemil il ªadad*	We're fully booked.
ارجع بعد شوية	*erga baªd showaiya*	Come back later.
فى أماكن بكرة.	*fi amaekin bokra*	We've got places tomorrow.
مقاسك إيه؟	*ma'aesak ay*	What size are you?
تحتاج...	*teHtaag...*	You need...
صورة فوتوغرافية	*Soora fotoghrafaya*	a photo
تأمين	*ta'meen*	insurance

✻ at the beach, river or pool

YOU MAY WANT TO SAY...

- Can I/we... | ...ممكن | **mom**kin...
  - swim here? | اعوم هنا؟ | aᵃoom **hena**
  - swim in the river? | اعوم فى النهر؟ | aᵃoom fin **nahr**

- Is it dangerous? | خطر؟ | **kha**Tar

- Is it safe for children? | امان للأطفال؟ | a'**maen** lil aT**faal**

- When is high tide? | امتى ميعاد المد؟ | **em**ta miᵃaed il mad

- Is the water clean? | المياة نظيفة؟ | il **mai**ya na**Dee**fa

- Where is the lifeguard? | فين عامل الأنقاذ؟ | fayn ᵃa**mil** il in**qaaz**

YOU MAY HEAR...

أحترس , خطر.	aH**teris kha**Tar	Be careful, it's dangerous.
التيار قوى.	it**tai**yaar 'awi	The current is very strong.
الرياح قوية.	ir**ri**yaH 'a**wi**ya	It's very windy.

sightseeing and activities

133

at the beach, river or pool

YOU MAY SEE...

ممنوع الغطس	*mamnooª il ghaTs*	no diving
ممنوع الجرى	*mamnooª il gari*	no running
خطر قنديل البحر	*khaTar 'andeel il baHr*	danger, jellyfish
ممكن العوم لما العلم يكون أحمر	*momkin il ªoom lama il ªalam yikoon aHmar*	you may swim if the flag is red
ممنوع العوم لما العلم يكون أسود	*mamnooª il ªoom lama il ªalam yikoon eswid*	you may not swim if the flag is black

sightseeing and activities

shops&services

shopping	136
paying	139
buying clothes and shoes	140
changing rooms	141
exchanges and refunds	142
bargaining	143
photography	144
at the tobacconist	145
buying alcohol	146
at the post office	146
at the bank	148
changing money	149
telephones	150
mobiles	151
the internet	152
faxes	152

* shopping

الخزنة	il **khaz**na	cashier
اجزاخانة	egzaghaena	pharmacy
احزية	aHzaya	footwear
انتيكات	antikaet	antiques
اوكازيون	okazyown	sales
بائع الجرائد	ba'**a** il garaiyed	newsagent's
بقالة	bi'aela	groceries
جزارة	gizara	butcher's
جواهرجى	gawahergi	jeweller's
حلاق	Hallaq	barber's
حلوانى	Halawaeni	cake shop
خاص بالأطفال	khaaS bil aTfaal	children's
خردوات	khorda**waet**	confectioner's
خضرى	kho**Dari**	greengrocer
ساعاتى	sa**a**aeti	watchmaker's
سماك	samaek	fishmonger's
سوبرماركت	**soo**permarket	supermarket
صندوق بريد	Sandoo' ba**reed**	post box
صيدلى	Saidali	chemist's
عروض خاصة	**a**orooD khaaSa	special offers
غرفة تغيير الملابس	**ghor**fit taghyeer il malaebis	fitting rooms
كوافير	kwa**fer**	hairdresser's
لعب	le**a**ab	toys
مأكولات صحية	ma'koolaet SaHaya	health foods
محل «اخدم نفسك»	ma**Hal** ikhdim nafsak	DIY shop
محل احزية	ma**Hal** aHzaya	shoe shop
محل اطعمة متنوعة	ma**Hal** aT**a**ama motanawe**a**a	delicatessen

محل تجاري	*maHal togaeri*	department store
محل تنظيف على الناشف	*maHal tanDeef ªala innaeshif*	dry-cleaners
محل لبيع البرفانات	*maHal libiaª il barfanaet*	perfumery
محل لبيع الورد	*maHal libiaª il ward*	florist's
مخبز	*makhbaz*	bakery
مركز مبيعات	*markaz mabiyªaet*	shopping centre
مصوراتي	*moSawaraati*	photographer's
مغلق	*moghlaq*	closed
مفتوح (طوال اليوم)	*maftooH (Tool il yowm)*	open (all day)
مكتبة	*maktaba*	bookshop
مكتبة	*maktaba*	stationer's
ملابس	*malaebis*	clothing
ملابس للرجال	*malaebis lirrigael*	men's clothing
ملابس للسيدات	*malaebis li sayeedaet*	women's clothing
منتجات جلدية	*montagaet gildaya*	leather goods
منتجات رياضية	*montagaet riyaDaya*	sports goods
منتجات كهربائية	*montagaet kahroba'aya*	electrical goods
نظاراتي	*naDaraati*	optician's
هدايا	*hedayya*	gifts
هدايا تزكارية	*hedayya tizkaraya*	souvenirs

shops and services

shopping

YOU MAY WANT TO SAY...

● Where is...	...فين	*fayn...*
the shopping centre?	المول؟	*il mowl*
● Where can I buy...	منين أشترى...	*minayn ashteri...*
a map?	خريطة؟	*khareeTa*
● I'd like ..., please.	من فضلك انا عايز/عايزة...	*min faDlak (to m)/faDlik (to f) ana ªayiz (m)/ªayza (f)...*
this one here	ده / دى	*da (m)/di (f)*
one of those	واحد من دول	*waHid min dowl*
two of those	أثنين من دول	*itnayn min dowl*
● Have you got...?	عندك...؟	*ªandak (to m)/ªandik (to f)...*
● How much does it/do they cost?	بكام...؟	*bikaem...*
● Can you write it down please?	ممكن تكتبها لى من فضلك؟	*momkin tiktebha li min faDlak (to m)/faDlik (to f)*
● I'm just looking.	أنا بأتفرج بس.	*ana batfarag bas*
● There's one in the window.	فى واحد فى الفترينة.	*fi waHid fil vatreena*
● I'll take it.	حا أشترى ده.	*Hashteri da*
● Can you...	ممكن...	*momkin...*
keep it for me?	تحجزها لى؟	*teHgizhaa li*
order it for me?	تطلبها لى؟	*toTlobhaa li*
● I need to think about it.	سيبنى أفكر.	*sebni afakkar*

YOU MAY HEAR...

أى خدمة؟	ay **khed**ma	Can I help you?
ثمنة خمسة وثمانين جنية.	ta**ma**noo **kham**sa wi tama**neen** gi**nee**	It costs L.E. 85.
أسف الصنف ده خلص.	**ae**sif iS**Sanf** da khe**liS**	I'm sorry, we've sold out.
ممكن نطلبه لك.	**mom**kin noT**loboo** liki	We can order it for you.

＊ paying

YOU MAY WANT TO SAY...

Where do I pay?	أدفع فين؟	**adfa**ª fayn
Do you take credit cards?	بتقبلوا كروت الأتمان؟	biti'ba**loo** ko**root** il 'i'ti**maen**
Can you wrap it, please?	ممكن تلفها لى؟	**mom**kin tili**fa**ha li
Can I have ... please?	من فضلك ممكن...	min **faD**lak (to m)/ **faD**lik (to f) **mom**kin...
a receipt	وصل؟	**waSl**
a bag	شنطة؟	**shan**Ta
my change	الفكة؟	il **fak**ka
Can I pay...	ممكن ادفع...	**mom**kin **adfa**ª...
in US Dollars	بالدولار؟	bid**do**laar
in Euros	باليورو؟	bil **yoo**ro
Sorry, I haven't got any change.	اسف معنديش فكة.	**ae**sif (m)/**as**fa (f) maªan**deesh fak**ka

shops and services

139

buying clothes and shoes

هدية؟	hedayya	Is it a gift?
تحبى الفها لك؟	teHebi alifahaelik	Do you want it wrapped?
عايز شنطة؟	^aayiz shanTa	Do you want a bag?
من فضلك ادفع هنا.	min faDlak edfa^a hena	Please pay here.
عندك فكة؟	^aandak fakka	Have you got any change?

* buying clothes and shoes
(see **clothes and shoe sizes**, page 25)

YOU MAY WANT TO SAY...

- Have you got... عندك... ^aandak (to m)/ ^aandik (to f)...

  a smaller size? مقاس أصغر؟ ma'aes aSghar

  a larger size? مقاس أكبر؟ ma'aes akbar

  other colours? الوان تانية؟ alwaen tanya

- I'm a size... أنا مقاس... ana ma'aes...

- I'm looking for... أنا عايز/عايزة... ana ^aayiz (m)/ ^aayza (f)...

  a hat برنيطة bornaeTa

  shorts شورت short

  sandals صندل Sandal

- Where are the changing rooms? فين غرفة تغيير الملابس؟ fayn ghorfit taghyeer il malaebis

shops and services

140

* changing rooms

- Can I try this on, please? | ممكن إقيس ده من فضلك؟ | *momkin a'ees da min faDlak* (to m)/ *faDlik* (to f)

- It doesn't fit. | مش مقاسي. | *mish ma'aesi*

- It's too big. | كبير قوى. | *kibeer awi*

- It's too small. | صغير قوى. | *Soghaiyar awi*

- It doesn't suit me. | مش لايق علية. | *mish layi' ªalaya*

تحبى تقيسى ده؟	*teHebi t'eesee da*	Would you like to try it/them on?
مقاسك إيه؟	*ma'aesik ay*	What size are you?
حا أجيب لك واحد تانى.	*Hageeblik waHid taeni*	I'll get you another one.
أسف دة أخير واحد.	*aesif da aekhir waHid*	Sorry, that's the last one.
لايق عليكى.	*layi' ªaleeki*	It suits/they suit you.

* exchanges and refunds

YOU MAY WANT TO SAY...

Excuse me...	...عن أذنك	*an iznak (to m)/ iznik (to f)...
there is something wrong	فى حاجة غلط	fi Haga ghalaT
this doesn't fit	مش مقاسى	mish ma'aesi
I'd like...	أنا عايز/عايزة...	ana *ayiz (m)/ *ayza (f)...
a refund	ترجع لى فلوسى	tirega* li filoosi
I'd like...	أنا عايز/عايزة...	ana *ayiz (m)/ *ayza (f)...
to return this	ارجع ده	araga* da
to change this	أغير ده	aghayar da

YOU MAY HEAR...

معاك...	ma*ak...	Have you got...
الأيصال؟	il iSaal	the receipt?
الضمان؟	iDDamaan	the guarantee?
أسف استرجاع الفلوس غير مسموح.	aesif istirga* il filoos mish masmooH	Sorry, we don't give refunds.
يمكن استبداله.	yomkin istibdaloo	You can exchange it.

✱ bargaining

● Part of the shopping experience in any Middle-Eastern market is price bargaining. This is done in good humour and shopkeepers expect you to have a go. However, it is important to remember that this is not acceptable in conventional shops!

YOU MAY WANT TO SAY...

● Is this your best price? | ده احسن سعر عندك؟ | *da aHsan seªr ªandak (to m)/ ªandik (to f)*

● It's too expensive. | السعر غالى جدا. | *isseªr ghaeli gedan*

● Is there a discount for cash? | فى تخفيض للبيدفع كاش؟ | *fi takhfeeD lili biyedfaª kash*

● I'll give you... | حا أديلك... | *Hadeelak (to m)/ Hadeelik (to f)...*

● That's my final offer! | أخر كلام! | *akheer kalaem*

shops and services

photography

* photography

● Can you print photos from a memory card?	ممكن طبع الصور من كارت الكاميرا؟	*momkin Tabª iSSowar min kart il kamera*
● When will it/they be ready?	حا تجهز امتى؟	*Hateghaz emta*
● Do you have an express service?	عندكم خدمة سريعة أكسبريس؟	*ªandokom khedma seriªa ekspress*
● How much does it cost...	بكام؟	*bikaem*
per print?	الصورة	*iSSoora*
● I'd like...	عايز/عايزة...	*ªayiz* (m)/*ªayza* (f)...
an 8MB memory card, please	كارت كاميرا ٨ ميجة من فضلك	*kart kamera tamanya mega min faDlak* (to m)/*faDlik* (to f)
● a disposable camera, please	كاميرا للأستعمال مرة واحدة من فضلك	*kamera lil isteªmael marra waHda min faDlak* (to m)/*faDlik* (to f)
● Do you do repairs?	فى صيانة للكاميرات؟	*fi Siyaana lil kameraat*

YOU MAY HEAR...

عايز الصور مقاس كام؟	*ayiz iSSowar ma'aes kaem	What size do you want your prints?
عايز الصور مات ولا بتلمع؟	*ayiz iSSowar mat wala bitelma*	Do you want them matt or gloss?
تعالى...	ta*ala...	Come back...
بكرة	bokra	tomorrow
بعد ساعة	ba*d sa*a	in an hour
عايز كارت كاميرة حجم أية؟	*ayiz kart kamera Hagm ay	What size memory card do you want?

✳ at the tobacconist

YOU MAY WANT TO SAY...

- Can I have a packet of... , please? — ممكن علبة ... من فضلك؟ — *momkin* *elba* ... *min faDlak* (to m)/ *faDlik* (to f)

- Do you sell... — بتبيع... — *bitbee*...
  - matches? — كبريت؟ — *kabreet*
  - lighters? — ولاعات؟ — *wala*aet*

- Do you sell cigars? — عندك سيجار؟ — *andak* (to m)/ *andik* (to f) *sigaar*

- Do you sell loose tobacco? — عندك طنباق؟ — *andak* (to m)/ *andik* (to f) *Tonbaaq*

shops and services

145

✳ buying alcohol

● You can buy alcohol from specialised grocers in countries where it is allowed, such as Lebanon, Egypt and Morocco.

YOU MAY WANT TO SAY...

● Have you got any...	عندك...	^aandak (to m)/ ^aandik (to f)...
local wine?	نبيذ محلي؟	nebeet maHali
imported beer?	بيرة مستوردة؟	beera mostawrada
● I'll take... please.	عايز/عايزة ... من فضلك.	^aayiz (m)/^aayza (f) ...min faDlak (to m) /faDlik (to f)
a bottle	زجاجة	zogaega
a pack	باكو	baeko

✳ at the post office

YOU MAY WANT TO SAY...

● A stamp for ... please.	طابع بريد ل ... من فضلك.	Tabi^a bareed li ... min faDlak (to m)/faDlik (to f)
Europe	اوروبا	oroba
America	امريكا	amreeka
● Five stamps please.	خمس طوابع من فضلك.	khamas Tawabi^a min faDlak (to m)/ faDlik (to f)

● Can I send this...   ...ممكن ارسل ده   *^amomkin arsil da...*
    by airmail?   بالبريد الجوى؟   *bil bareed iggawi*

    by sea?   بالبريد البحرى؟   *bil bareed il baHari*

● I want to send this parcel by Express post.   عايز/ عايزة ابعث الطرد ده بالبريد المستعجل.   *^aayiz (m)/^aayza (f) ab^aat iTTard da bil bareed il mista^agil*

● It contains...   ...يحتوى على   *yaHtawi ^aala...*
    something valuable   شىء ثمين   *shi' thameen*
    something fragile   شىء قابل للكسر   *shi' qaabil lil kasr*

● Can I have a receipt, please?   ممكن إيصال من فضلك؟   *momkin iySal min faDlak (to m)/ faDlik (to f)*

YOU MAY HEAR...

الخطاب مرسل لمن؟   *il kheTaab morsal limeen*   Where is it going to?

كروت بريد او خطابات؟   *koroot bareed aw kheTabaat*   For postcards or letters?

ضعه على الميزان من فضلك.   *Do^ao ^aala il mizaen min faDlak (to m)/ faDlik (to f)*   Put it on the scales, please.

ماذا فى داخل المظروف؟   *maeza fi daekhil il maZroof*   What's in it?

برجاء كتابة شهادة الجمرك.   *bi ragaa' kitaebit shahaedit il gomrok*   Please complete the customs form.

✳ at the bank

YOU MAY WANT TO SAY...

- Excuse me, where's the foreign exchange counter?

  عن إذنك فين مكتب تغيير العملة؟

  ª an iznak (to m)/ *iznik* (to f) *fayn maktab taghyeer il oªomla*

- Is there a cashpoint machine here?

  فى الة سحب فلوس هنا؟

  fi aelit saHb filoos hena

- The cashpoint machine has eaten my card.

  الة سحب الفلوس اكلت الكارت.

  aelit saHb il filoos akalit il kart

- I've forgotten my pin number.

  نسيت الرقم السرى.

  niseet irraqam isseri

- I'd like to...

  عايز/عايزة...

  ª ayiz (m)/*ª ayza* (f)...

  withdraw some money

  اسحب شوية فلوس

  asHab showaiyit filoos

- Has my money arrived yet?

  فلوسى وصلت؟

  filoosi waSalit

YOU MAY HEAR...

بطاقتك الشخصية من فضلك.	*biTa'tak ishshakhSaya min faDlak*	Your ID, please.
جواز سفرك من فضلك.	*gawaez safarik min faDlik*	Your passport, please.
اسمك إيه؟	*ismak ay*	What's your name?

shops and services

148

* changing money

I'd like to change ..., please.	من فضلك انا عايز/عايزة أغير...	min **faD**lak (to m)/**faD**lik (to f) *a***ayiz** (m)/*a***ayza** (f) a**ghai**yar...
travellers' cheques	الشيكات السياحية	ishshi**kaet** issiya**Haya**
one hundred pounds	مائة جنية	meet gi**nee**
Can I get money out on my credit card?	ممكن اصرف فلوس بكارت الأتمان؟	**mom**kin a**S**rif fi**loos** bi**kart** il 'i'ti**maen**
What's the rate today...	ما هى قيمة ... النهار ده.	ma **haya** qee**mit** ... ina**har**da
for the pound?	الجنية	ig**gi**nay
for the dollar?	الدولار	id**do**laar
for the euro?	اليورو	il **yoo**ro

كام؟	**kaem**	How much?
جواز السفر من فضلك.	ga**waez** issa**far** min **faD**lak	Passport, please.
وقع هنا من فضلك.	**waqa**a **he**na min **faD**lik	Sign here, please.

shops and services

149

* telephones

telephones

YOU MAY WANT TO SAY...

Where's the (nearest) phone?	فين (اقرب) تليفون؟	fayn (a'rab) tilifown
I'd like to...	عايز/عايزة...	ªayiz (m)/ªayza (f)...
buy a phone card	أشترى كارت تليفون	ashteri kart tilifown
call England	أكلم أنجلترا	akalim ingiltera
make a reverse charge call	احول ثمن المكالمة للمستلم	aHawil taman il mokalma lil moostalim
The number is...	الرقم هو...	irraqam howa...
How much does it cost per minute?	الدقيقة بكام؟	idd'ee'a bikaem
What's the area code for...?	ما هو رقم النداء المحلى...؟	ma howa raqam inneeda' il maHali...
What's the country code?	ما هو رقم النداء الدولى؟	ma howa raqam inneeda' iddawli
How do I get an outside line?	كيف احصل على خط خارجى؟	kaifa aHSol ªala khaT khaerigi
It's ... speaking.	معاك...	maªaek (to m)/ maªaeki (to f)...
Can I speak to...?	ممكن اكلم...؟	momkin akalim...
I'll ring back.	حاتكلم تانى.	Hatkalim taeni
It's a bad line.	الخط وحش.	il khaT weHish
I've been cut off.	الخط أنقطع.	il khaT in'aTaª

shops and services

YOU MAY HEAR...

الو.	*alow*	Hello.
مين بيتكلم؟	*meen biyetkalim*	Who's calling?
اسف مش موجود.	*aesif mish mawgood* (m)/*mawgooda* (f)	Sorry, he/she's not here.
لحظة من فضلك.	*laHZa min faDlik*	Just a moment.
النمرة مشغولة.	*innemra mashghoola*	It's engaged.
مفيش حد بيرد.	*mafeesh Had birod*	There's no answer.
ح تنتظر؟	*HatantaZir*	Do you want to hold?

✳ mobiles

YOU MAY WANT TO SAY...

- Have you got...   عندك...   *ᵃandak* (to m)/ *ᵃandik* (to f)

  a charger for this phone?   شاحن للتليفون ده؟   *shaHin lit tilifown da*

  a SIM card for the local network?   كارت لشركة الموبايل؟   *kart li shirkit il mowbail*

- Can I/we hire a mobile?   ممكن نأجر موبيل؟   *momkin na'agar mowbail*

- What's the tariff?   بكام؟   *bikaem*

- Are text messages included?   شامل رسائل التكست؟   *shaemil rasaeyil ittekst*

✳ the internet

YOU MAY WANT TO SAY...

- Is there an internet café near here?

  فيه انترنت كافية قريب؟

  fi internet kafay oraiyib

- It's very slow.

  بطيء جداً.

  baTee' gedan

- Can you...
  print this?

  ممكن...
  اطبع ده؟

  momkin...
  aTbaᵃ da

- Can I...
  use my memory stick?

  ممكن...
  استخدم الذاكرة المتنقلة؟

  momkin...
  astakhdim izzaekera il motanaqela

YOU MAY SEE...

أسم المستخدم	*ism il mostakhdim*	username
كلمة السر	*kilmit isser*	password
إضغط هنا	*eDghaT hena*	click here

✳ faxes

YOU MAY WANT TO SAY...

- What's your fax number?

  ما هو رقم الفاكس عندك؟

  ma howa raqam il faks ᵃandak (to m)/ᵃandik (to f)

- Can you send this fax for me, please?

  ممكن تبعث لى الفاكس ده من فضلك؟

  momkin tebᵃat li il faks da min faDlak (to m)/faDlik (to f)

- How much is it?

  بكام؟

  bikaem

at the chemist's	154
at the doctor's	155
describing your symptoms	156
medical complaints and conditions	158
parts of the body	161
at the dentist's	163
emergencies	164
police	166
reporting crime	167

health&safety

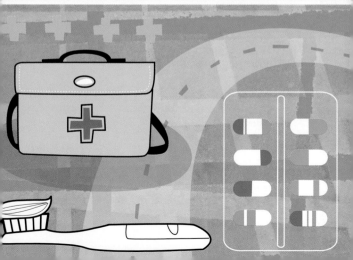

✳ at the chemist's

● Chemist's, or pharmacies, as they're called in most Arab countries, usually have a sign outside showing a goblet and a snake. Many drugs which are available only on prescription in Britain may be obtained over the counter.

YOU MAY WANT TO SAY...

● Have you got something...

عندك علاج لـ...

andak (to m)/ andik (to f) ilaeg...

  for sunburn?

حروق الشمس؟

li Horoo' ishshams

  for diarrhoea?

الاسهال؟

lil is-hael

● I need some ... please.

عايز/عايزة ... من فضلك.

ayiz (m)/ayza (f) ... min faDlak (to m)/faDlik (to f)

  aftersun

كريم بعد الشمس

kraym bad ishshams

  aspirin

اسبرين

asbireen

  baby wipes

مساحات للأطفال

massaHaet lil aTfaal

  condoms

كبوت

kaboot

  insect repellent

طارد للحشرات

Taarid lil Hasharaat

  plasters

بلاستر

blaster

  sanitary towels

فوط صحية

fowaT SaHaya

  shampoo

شامبو

shampoo

  tampons

صمامات قطنية للسيدات

Samamaat oTnaya lis sayidaat

health and safety

tissues	مناديل ورق (كلينيكس)	mana**deel** wara' (klee**neks**)
toilet paper	ورق تواليت	wara' twa**lit**
toothpaste	معجون أسنان	ma**ª**goon issi**naen**
travel sickness pills	حبوب ضد دوخة السفر	Ho**boob** Ded **dow**khit issa**far**
● Can you make up this prescription, please?	ممكن تركيب الدواء ده من فضلك؟	**mom**kin ter**keeb** id**dawa da** min **faD**lak (to m)/ **faD**lik (to f)

YOU MAY HEAR...

| اخذت الدواء ده قبل كده؟ | ak**hadt** il **dawa da** abl **ke**da | Have you taken this before? |
| معاك روشتة؟ | ma**ª**aek ro**shetta** | Have you got a prescription? |

✳ at the doctor's

(see **medical complaints and conditions**, page 158)

YOU MAY WANT TO SAY...

● I need a doctor (who speaks English).	عايز/عايزة دكتور (بيتكلم انجليزي).	**ª**ayiz (m)/**ª**ayza (f) dok**towr** (biyet**ka**lim in**glee**zi)
● Can I make an appointment for...	ممكن اخذ ميعاد...	**mom**kin a**khod** mi**ª**aed...
today?	النهارده؟	inna**har**da
tomorrow?	بكره؟	**bok**ra

● I've run out of my medication.	الدواء خلص.	*iddawa kheliS*
● I'm on medication for...	الدواء للعلاج ضد....	*iddawa lil ªilaeg Ded...*
● I've had a ... jab.	اطعمت ضد....	*iTaªamt Ded...*
tetanus	التتنيوس	*ittetnyows*
typhoid	التيفود	*ittaifood*
rabies	عضة الكلب	*ªaDit il kalb*
● He/She has had a ... vaccination.	هو/هى أتطعمت ضد....	*howa/haya iTaªamit Ded...*
polio	البوليو	*il polyo*
measles	الحصبة	*il HaSbah*
● Can I have a receipt for my health insurance, please?	ممكن إيصال لشركة التامين من فضلك؟	*momkin iSaal li shirkit itta'meen min faDlak (to m)/ faDlik (to f)*

✳ describing your symptoms

● To tell a doctor or pharmacist where a pain is, you can simply point and say *fi aʼlam hena* (it hurts here).

describing your symptoms

YOU MAY WANT TO SAY...

I don't feel well.	أنا تعبان/أنا تعبانة.	*ana ta*^a*baen* (m)/ *ta*^a*baena* (f)
It hurts here.	فى الم هنا.	*fi a'lam hena*
My stomach hurts.	معدتى بتوجعنى.	*ma*^a*deti bitewga*^a*ni*
My head hurts.	راسى بتوجعنى.	*raa*si *bitewga*^a*ani*
I've got...	عندى...	^a*andi*
diarrhoea	الاسهال	*is-hael*
swollen glands	ورم في الغدد	*wa*ram *fi il gho*dad
I'm dizzy.	اشعر بالدوخة.	*ash*^a*or bid*dowkha
I feel sick.	عايز استفرغ.	^a*ayiz* (m)/^a*ayza* (f) *asta*fragh
I can't...	مش قادر...	*mish 'ae*dir...
breathe properly	اتنفس بسهولة	*atna*fis bisihoola
sleep properly	انام بسهولة	*anaem bisihoola*
My nose is bleeding.	مناخيرى بتنزل دم.	*manakhee*ri bitnazil *dam*
My arm is bleeding.	ذراعى بينزل دم.	*deera*^a*i biye*nazil *dam*
I've cut/burnt myself.	جرحت نفسى/حرقت نفسى.	*ga*raHt *naf*si/ *Ha*ra't *naf*si
I've been sick.	استفرغت.	*ista*fraght

health and safety

157

* medical complaints and conditions

YOU MAY WANT TO SAY...

- I'm...
  عندي...
  ^aandi...

  arthritic
  التهاب في المفاصل
  iltihaeb fil mafaaSil

  asthmatic
  ربو
  rabu

  diabetic
  سكر
  sokkar

  epileptic
  صرع
  Sara^a

- I've got...
  عندي...
  ^aandi...

  high/low blood pressure
  ضغط دم عالي/واطي
  DaghT dam ^aaeli/waaTi

  a heart condition
  القلب
  il 'alb

- I'm...
  أنا...
  ana...

  pregnant
  حامل
  Haemil

  blind
  أعمى
  a^ama

  deaf
  أطرش
  aTrash

- I use a wheelchair.
  استعمل كرسي المعاقين.
  asta^amil korsi lilmo^aaqeen

- I have difficulty walking.
  بامشي بصعوبة.
  bamshi biSo^aooba

- I've got AIDS.
  أنا عندي أيدز.
  ana ^aandi aydz

- I'm allergic to...
  عندي حساسية ضد...
  ^aandi Hasasaya Ded...

  nuts
  المكسرات
  il mikassaraat

  penicillin
  البنسلين
  il bansileen

  dairy products
  منتجات الالبان
  montagaet il albaen

  eggs
  البيض
  il bayD

YOU MAY HEAR...

الالم فين؟	il 'alam fayn	Where does it hurt?
فى الم هنا؟	fi 'alam hena	Does it hurt here?
بتاخذ دواء؟	bitaekhod dawa	Are you on medication?
عندك حساسية ضد اى شىء؟	ªandak Hasasaya Ded ay sha'	Are you allergic to anything?
لازم أقيس الحرارة.	laezim 'a'ees il Haraara	I need to take your temperature.
من فضلك أقلع ملابسك.	min faDlak i'laª malabsak	Get undressed, please.
نامى على السرير من فضلك	naem ªala issereer min faDlak	Lie down here, please.
مفيش حاجة تخوف.	mafeesh Haga tekhawif	It's nothing serious.
عندك التهاب.	ªandak iltihaeb	You've got an infection.
فى التهاب.	fi iltihaeb	It's infected.
محتاج عينة...	miHtaeg ªayenit...	I need a ... sample.
دم	dam	blood
بول	bowl	urine
براز	booraaz	stool
محتاج أشعة.	miHtaeg asheªa	You need an X-ray.
حا أديلك حقنة.	Hadeelak Ho'nah	I'm going to give you an injection.
عندك حساسية ضد البنسلين؟	ªandak Hasasaya Ded il bansileen	Are you allergic to pencillin?

medical complaints

لازم تستريح.	*laezim tisteraiyaH*	You must rest.
لاتشرب الكحول.	*laetashrab alkoHol*	You mustn't drink alcohol.
لازم تزور دكتور بعد ما ترجع بلدك.	*laezim tizoor doktowr baªd matergaª baladak*	You should see a doctor when you go home.
لازم تروح مستشفى.	*laezim tiroH mostashfa*	You need to go to hospital.
قصعت...	*'aSaªt...*	You've sprained your...
كعب الرجل	*kaªb irregl*	ankle
كسرت...	*kasart...*	You've broken your...
ضلوعك	*Doolooªak*	ribs
عندك...	*ªandak...*	You've got...
أنفلونزا	*infloowenza*	flu
أزمة قلبية	*'azma 'albaya*	It's a heart attack.
لازم ترجعا تزورنا كمان ثلاثة أيام	*laezim tergaª tizorna kamaen talat ayaem*	You must come back in three days' time.

* parts of the body

ankle	كعب الرجل	*ka^ab irregl*
appendix	مصران	*moSraan*
arm	زراع	*dira^a*
artery	شريان	*shoryaen*
back	ظهر	*Dahr*
bladder	مثانة	*mathaena*
blood	دم	*dam*
body	جسم	*gism*
bone	عظم	*^aaDm*
bottom	ارداف	*'ardaef*
bowels	امعاء	*am^aa'*
breast	ثدى	*thadi*
chest	صدر	*Sadr*
collar bone	عظمة الرقبة	*^aaDmit il ra'aba*
ear	أذن	*wedn*
elbow	كوع	*koo^a*
eye	عين	*^aayn*
face	وجة	*wagh*
finger	صباع	*Sooba^a*
foot	قدم	*'adam*
genitals	اعضاء تناسلية	*'^aDa' tanaesolaya*
gland	غدة	*ghodda*
hand	يد	*yed*
head	رأس	*raas*
heart	قلب	*'alb*
heel	كعب	*ka^ab*
jaw	فك	*fak*
joint	مفصل	*mafSal*

health and safety

161

parts of the body

kidney	كلوة	*kilwa*
knee	ركبة	*rokba*
leg	رجل	*regl*
ligament	وتر	*watar*
liver	كبد	*kebd*
lung	رئة	*re'ah*
mouth	فم	*fam*
muscle	عضلة	*ªaDala*
nail	ظفر	*Dofr*
neck	رقبة	*ra'aba*
nerve	عصب	*ªaSab*
nose	مناخير	*manakheer*
penis	عضو الذكورة	*ªoDow iz zokoora*
rib	ضلع	*Delª*
shoulder	كتف	*ketf*
skin	جلد	*geld*
spine	العمود الفقرى	*il ªamood il fa'ri*
stomach	المعدة	*il meªda*
tendon	رباط العضلة	*robaaT il ªaDala*
testicle	الخاصية	*il khaSya*
thigh	الفخد	*il fakhd*
throat	الزور	*izzowr*
toe	صباع الرجل	*Soobaª irregl*
tongue	لسان	*lisaen*
tonsils	لوز	*lewaz*
tooth	سن	*sin*
vagina	رحم	*raHim*
vein	عرق	*ªer'*
wrist	رسخ	*raskh*

✳ at the dentist's

YOU MAY WANT TO SAY...

● I need a dentist (who speaks English).	عايز دكتور سنان (بيتكلم أنجليزى).	ᵃayiz (m)/ᵃayza (f) doktowr sinaen (biyetkalim ingleezi)
● It (really) hurts.	الألم شديد جداً.	il 'alam shedeed gedan
● It's my wisdom tooth.	ضرس العقل.	Ders il ᵃa'l
● I've lost...	فقدت...	faqadt...
a filling	الحشو	il Hashw
a crown/cap	التاج	ittaeg

YOU MAY HEAR...

أفتح الفم على الأخر.	eftaH il fam ᵃala il aekhir	Open wide.
أقفل الفك.	i'fil il fak	Close your jaws together.
تحتاج أشعة.	teHtaeg asheᵃa	You need an x-ray.
أنت حامل؟	inti Haemil	Are you pregnant?
لازم اخلعة.	laezim akhlaᵃo	I'll have to take it out.
حا أديلك...	Hadeelak...	I'm going to give you...
حقنة	Ho'na	an injection
حشو مؤقت	Hashw mow'aqat	a temporary filling

health and safety

* emergencies

● To find out the emergency numbers for the country you are visiting before you travel, check with the relevant consulate.

YOU MAY SEE...

أسعافات أولية	is°afaet awalaya	first aid
خدمات الطوارىء	khadamaet iTTawaari'	emergency services
دكتور/دكتورة	doktowr/doktowra	doctor
رج قبل الأستخدام	rog 'abl il istikhdaem	shake before use
سم	sim	poison
طريقة الأستخدام	Tareeqit il istikhdaem	instructions for use
عيادة	°iyaada	clinic
عيادة خاصة	°iyaada khaSa	private clinic
قسم الحوادث والطوارىء	qesm il Hawaedis wil Tawaari'	Accident and Emergency
للأستخدام الخارجى فقط	lil istikhdaem il khaerigi faqaT	for external use only
مستشفى	mostashfa	hospital
ممرض/ممرضة	momarriD/momarriDa	nurse
مواعيد العيادة	mow°eed il °yaeda	surgery times

YOU MAY WANT TO SAY...

I need...	...انا محتاج/محتاجة	*ana meHtaeg* (m)/ *meHtaega* (f)...
a doctor	دكتور/دكتورة	*doktowr* (m)/ *doktowra* (f)
an ambulance	إسعاف	*isªaef*
the fire brigade	المطافىء	*il maTaafi*
the police	البوليس	*il bolees*
Immediately!	فوراً!	*fawran*
It's very urgent!	بسرعة!	*bisorªa*
Help!	ساعدونى!	*saªdooni*
Please help us.	من فضلكم ساعدونى.	*min faDlokom saªdooni*
There's a fire!	فى حريقة!	*fi Haree'a*
There's been an accident.	فى حادثة.	*fi Hadsa*
I have to use the phone.	لازم استعمل التليفون.	*laezim astaªmil ittilifown*
I'm lost.	فقدت الطريق.	*faqadt iTTaree'*
I've lost my...	فقدت ...	*faqadt...*
son	أبنى	*ibni*
daughter	أبنتى	*binti*
Stop!	قف!	*qef*

YOU MAY HEAR...

أنت فين؟	*enta fayn*	Where are you?
عنوانك إيه؟	*ªenwaenak ay*	What's your address?

health and safety

165

police

* police

YOU MAY WANT TO SAY...

● Sorry, I didn't realise it was against the law.	أسف /أسفة ما كنتش أعرف ان ده ضد القانون.	*aesif* (m)/*asfa* (f) *makontish aªraf in da Ded il qanoon*
● Here are my documents.	إتفضل مستنداتي.	*itfaDal mostanadaeti*
● I haven't got my passport on me.	الباسبور مش معايا.	*il basbor mish maªaya*
● I don't understand.	مش فاهم/فاهمة.	*mish faehim* (m)/ *fahma* (f)
● I'm innocent.	أنا بريء.	*ana baree'* (m)/ *baree' a* (f)
● I need a lawyer (who speaks English).	عايز/عايزة محامي (بيتكلم أنجليزي).	*ªayiz* (m)/*ªayza* (f) *moHaemi* (*biyetkalim ingleezi*)
● I want to contact my...	عايز/عايزة أتصل ب...	*ªayiz* (m)/*ªayza* (f) *ateSil bi...*
embassy	السفارة	*issifara*
consulate	القنصلية	*il 'onSolaya*

YOU MAY HEAR...

لازم تدفع غرامة.	*laezim tedfaª gharaama*	You'll have to pay a fine.
مستنداتك من فضلك.	*mostanadaetak min faDlak*	Your documents please.

health and safety

166

معاك بطاقة أو باسبور؟	ma^aak biTa'a aw basbor	Have you got an ID card or passport?
تعالى معابا.	ta^aaela ma^aaya	Come with me.

✳ reporting crime

YOU MAY WANT TO SAY...

● I want to report a theft.

عايز/عايزة أبلغ عن حادثة سرقة.

^aayiz (m)/^aayza (f) abalagh ^aan Hadsit ser'ah

● My purse/wallet has been stolen.

محفظتى أتسرقت.

maHfaZti itsara'it

● My passport has been stolen.

جواز سفرى أتسرق.

gawaez safari itsara'

● My mobile phone has been stolen.

موبيلى أتسرق.

mowbaili itsara'

● Our car has been broken into.

أقتحموا العربية.

iqtaHamoo il ^aarabaya

● Our car has been stolen.

عربيتنا أتسرقت.

^aarabiyitna itsara'it

● I've lost my...
    credit cards

فقدت...
بطاقات الأئتمان

faqadt...
biTa'aat il 'i'timaen

    luggage

الشنط

ishshonaaT

● I've been attacked.

اعتدو علي

^atadoo ^aalaya

YOU MAY HEAR...

حصلت أمتى؟	*HaSalit emta*	When did it happen?
فين؟	*fayn*	Where?
أية اللى حصل؟	*ay illi HaSal*	What happened?
شكلة/شكلها أية؟	*shaklo/shaklaha ay*	What did he/she look like?
شكلهم أية؟	*shaklohom ay*	What did they look like?

YOU MAY WANT TO SAY...

- It happened...
  - five minutes ago
  - last night
  - on the beach

  حصل...
  من خمس دقائق
  أمبارح بالليل
  على الشاطىء

  HaSal...
  min khamas da'aye'
  imbaeriH bilayl
  ªala ishshaaTi'

- He/she had blonde hair.

  شعرة/شعرها ذهبى.

  shaªro/shaªraha dahabi

- He/she had a knife.

  كان معاه/معاها سكينة.

  kaen maªah/maªaha sikeena

- He/She was...
  - tall

  - young

  هو /هى...
  طويل/ طويلة

  شاب/شابة

  howa/haya...
  Taweel (m)/
  Taweela (f)
  shaeb (m)/
  shaeba (f)

- He/She was wearing...
  - jeans
  - a red shirt

  كان لابس/كانت لابسة...
  بنطلون جينز
  قميص أحمر

  kaen laebis/kaenit labsa...
  bantalown jeenz
  'amees aHmar

basic grammar

There are two types of Arabic: classical, which is the written form, and colloquial, the spoken language, which varies from country to country. In this book we are using the Egyptian colloquial form which is the most widely understood in all 23 Arab countries. The basic rules of grammar apply wherever you are.

✳ nouns

Arabic nouns are either masculine or feminine. As a rule, feminine nouns end in -a, or less commonly -at. Often the feminine form of a word is formed by adding one of these endings to the masculine, e.g:

MASCULINE		FEMININE		
طالب	*Taalib*	طالبة	*Taaliba*	student
مدرس	*moddarris*	مدرسة	*moddarrisa*	teacher

However, there are many 'irregular' feminine nouns, such as:

بنت	*bint*	girl
أم	*om*	mother

Names of towns and countries are nearly always feminine.

✻ plurals

In Arabic the ending of nouns change in the plural. For 'regular' nouns you add -*een* to masculine nouns, and -*aet* to feminine nouns, e.g:

MASCULINE		FEMININE		
مهندس *mohandis*		مهندسة *mohandisa*	engineer	
مهندسين *mohandiseen*		مهندسات *mohandisaet*	engineers	

'Irregular' nouns have no set rules for forming the plural - it's a matter of learning them as you go along, e.g:

SINGULAR		PLURAL		
بصلة *baSala*	onion	بصل *baSal*	onions	
شنطة *shanTa*	bag	شنط *shonaT*	bags	

There's a special plural for when you are referring to two of something: you add بن (-*ayn*) to the end of masculine words, and تين (-*tayn*) to feminine ones, e.g:

SINGULAR		PLURAL		
ليلة *layla*	night	ليلتين *layltayn*	two nights	
سرير *sereer*	bed	سريرين *sereerayn*	two beds	

✳ articles (a, an, the)

The definite article 'the' in Arabic is ال (*il* or *al*). This is the same for masculine and feminine, singular and plural. There is no indefinite article 'a' or 'an'. Meanings often depend on the position of ال - and whether it is used at all, e.g.

ARTICLES		
بيت	*bayt*	a house
البيت	*il bayt*	the house
البيت الكبير	*il bayt il kibeer*	the big house
البيت كبير	*il bayt kibeer*	the house is big

✳ possessives (my, your, his, her, etc.)

Arabic adds a range of endings to nouns to denote possession:

MASCULINE		FEMININE		
ى	*–i*	تى	*–ti*	my
اك	*–ak*	يك	*–ik*	your (s)
و	*–o*	ها	*–ha*	his/her/its
نا	*–na*	تنا	*–tna*	our
كم	*–kom*	كم	*–kom*	your (pl)
هم	*–hom*	تهم	*–t-hom*	their

For example:

شنطتى	*shanTiti*	my bag
باسبورو	*basboro*	his passport

If the 'possessive' noun is accompanied by an adjective, this must be preceded by the definite article (*il/al*), e.g:

كتاب كبير	*kitaeb kibeer*	a big book
كتابى الكبير	*kitaebi il kibeer*	my big book

✳ adjectives

In Arabic, adjectives come after the noun. They have different endings according to whether the noun is masculine or feminine, singular or plural. For specific nouns, e.g. the bus, the article *il* must be used before both the adjective and the noun, e.g:

الأوتوبيس الكبير   *il otobees il kibeer* (m)   the big bus
الطيارة الكبيرة   *il Taiyaara il kibeera* (f)   the big aeroplane

For 'regular' adjectives, you add *-a* to the masculine singular to make the feminine singular.

SINGULAR		
مطعم رخيص	*maTªam* (m) *rekheeS*	cheap restaurant
شنطة خضرة	*shanTa* (f) *khaDra*	green bag

For plurals, when referring to things (as opposed to people), adjectives have the feminine singular ending, e.g:

PLURAL		
مطاعم رخيصة	*maTaaªim rekheeSa*	cheap restaurants
شنط خضراء	*shonaT khaDra*	green bags

When referring to people, the endings are *-een* for masculine, *-aat* or *-aet* for feminine, e.g:

SINGULAR		
ولد صغير	*walad Soghaiyar*	small boy
صبية طويلة	*Sabiya taweela*	tall girl

اولاد صغيرين	aewl*aed* Soghaiy*ereen*	small boys
صبايا طويلات	Sabaiya taweel*aet*	tall girls

✳ subject pronouns (I, you, he, she, it, etc.)

Subject pronouns are often omitted in colloquial Arabic; usually it is clear from the context who or what is being referred to. They're sometimes used to give special emphasis.

PRONOUNS		
انا	*ana*	I
انت	*inta*	you (m. sing)
انت	*inti*	you (f. sing)
هو	*howa*	he/it
هى	*haya*	she
احنا	*iHna*	we
انتم	*intom*	you (pl)
هم	*homma*	they

Object pronouns (me, him, her, it, etc.) are the same as the subject pronouns.

✳ demonstratives (this, that)

Arabic doesn't differentiate between 'this' and 'that' but there are masculine and feminine forms, depending on the gender of the noun. There is also a plural form.

ده	*da*	this/that (m)
دى	*di*	this/that (f)
دول	*dowl*	these/those

✳ verbs

There is no infinitive (to…) in Arabic, so in the dictionary at the end of this book, verbs are given in the 'he' and 'she' present tense form.

✳ regular verbs

Arabic verbs have different forms according to the subject of the verb and the tense. They are formed from a 'root' of three letters, and the different forms are made by changing the beginning, middle and/or end of the root.

For example, the root of 'travel' is the letters س ف ر (s, f, r). Once you know the root letters of a verb, you can work out

PRESENT TENSE		
اسافر	*asaefir*	I travel
تسافر	*tisaefir*	you (m. sing) travel
تسافرى	*tisafri*	you (f. sing) travel
يسافر	*yisaefir*	he/it travels
تسافر	*tisaefir*	she/it travels
نسافر	*nisaefir*	we travel
تسافروا	*tisafroo*	you (pl) travel
يسافرو	*yisafroo*	they travel

PAST TENSE

سافرت	*safirt*	I travelled
سافرت	*safirt*	you (m. sing) travelled
سافرتى	*safirti*	she (f. sing) travelled
سافر	*safir*	he/it travelled
سافرت	*safrit*	she/it travelled
سافرنا	*safirna*	we travelled
سافرتم	*safirtom*	you (pl) travelled
سافروا	*safroo*	they travelled

FUTURE TENSE

حا اسافر	*Hasaefir*	I will travel
حا تسافر	*Hatsaefir*	you (m. sing) will travel
حا تسافرى	*Hatsafri*	she (f. sing) will travel
حا يسافر	*Haisaefir*	he/it will travel
حا تسافر	*Hatsaefir*	she/it will travel
حا نسافر	*Hansaefir*	we will travel
حا تسافروا	*Hatsafroo*	you (pl) will travel
حا يسافروا	*Haisafroo*	they will travel

✳ irregular verbs

There are a number of 'irregular' verbs in Arabic, which
do not follow the pattern above. They have to be learned
separately.

✱ the verb 'to be'

Arabic has no verb 'to be'; the subject is followed by the rest of the sentence, without a verb, e.g:

| أنا طالب | *ana Taalib* | I am a student |
| هو دكتور | *howa doktowr* | he is a doctor |

To say 'there is' or 'there are', use the word فى (*fi*), e.g:

| فى كرسى | *fi korsi* | there is a chair |
| فى تذاكر | *fi tazaekir* | there are tickets |

To put something in the past tense, use the following:

كنت	*kont*	I was
كنت	*kont*	you (m. sing) were
كنتى	*konti*	you (f. sing) were
كان	*kaen*	he/it was
كانت	*kaenit*	she/it was
كنا	*konna*	we were
كنتم	*kontom*	you (pl) were
كانوا	*kaenoo*	they were

For example:

| كان كبير | *kaen kibeer* | it was big |
| كانوا جعانين | *kaeno gaªaneen* | they were hungry |

✳ the verb 'to have'

Arabic has no verb 'to have', either. Instead, one of two words can be used to indicate possession. These are عند (ᵃand), meaning 'possess', and مع (maᵃ) meaning 'have with…(at the present time)'. They are used with a suffix:

عندى	ᵃ**andi**	معايا	maᵃ**aiya**	I have
عندك	ᵃ**andak**	معاك	maᵃ**ak**	you (m. sing) have
عندك	ᵃ**andik**	معاكى	maᵃ**aki**	you (f. sing) have
عنده	ᵃ**ando**	معاة	ma**ᵃa**	he/it has
عندها	ᵃ**andaha**	معاها	maᵃ**aha**	she/it has
عندنا	ᵃ**andena**	معانا	maᵃ**ena**	we have
عندكم	ᵃ**andokom**	معاكم	maᵃ**akom**	you (pl) have
عندهم	ᵃ**andohom**	معاهم	maᵃ**ahom**	they have

For example:

عندى عربية	ᵃ**andi** ᵃara**baya**	I own a car.
معايا عربية	maᵃ**aiya** ᵃara**baya**	I've got a car with me.

✳ *momkin*

Perhaps one of the most useful words to learn in Arabic is ممكن (*momkin*). Used with the present tense of any verb, it means 'can I?', 'is it permitted?', or even 'please may I have…?', e.g:

ممكن اركن هنا؟	**momkin** *arkin hena* Can I park here?
ممكن مخدة من فضلك؟	**momkin** *makhadda min faDlak*
	Please may I have a pillow?

* negatives

The negative in Arabic is formed in one of two main ways. With verbs, *ma-* is put in front of the verb, and *-sh* after it, e.g:

فى كلب	*fi kalb*	there is a dog
مفيش كلب	*mafeesh kalb*	there is no dog

With adjectives and adverbs مش (*mish*) is put before the word, e.g:

ده ممكن	*da momkin*	this is possible
ده مش ممكن	*da mish momkin*	this is not possible

* questions

Questions in written Arabic end with a back-to-front question mark: ؟. To indicate a question in speech, usually the voice simply rises at the end of the sentence. However, you can also make a sentence into a question by putting هل (*hael*) at the beginning:

الجو حلو	*iggaw Helw*	the weather is good
هل الجو حلو	*hael iggaw Helw*	is the weather good?

Other question words can come at the beginning or end of a sentence, e.g:

حا تسافرى امتى؟	*Hatsafri emta*	
	or	when will you travel?
امتى حا تسافرى؟	*emta Hatsafri*	

English – Arabic Dictionary

Arabic nouns are given with their gender in brackets: (m) for masculine and (f) for feminine, (m/f) for those which can be either, (pl) for plural.

Adjectives which have different endings for masculine and feminine are shown like this: *modmin/modmina*. See **basic grammar**, page 169 for further explanation.

There's a list of **car parts** on page 64 and **parts of the body** on page 161. See also the **menu reader** on page 106, and **numbers** on page 16.

A

abroad فى الخارج *fil khaerig*
to accept: he/she accepts يقبل/تقبل *ye'bal/te'bal*
accident حادثة *Haedsa* (f)
accommodation سكن *sakan* (m)
ache ألم *alam* (m)
across (opposite) قدام *'uddaem*
actor ممثل *momasil*
actress ممثلة *momasilla*
adaptor محول *moHawil* (m)
addicted مدمن/مدمنة *modmin/modmina*
address عنوان *'enwaen* (m)
admission charge سعر الدخول *se'ar iddokhool* (m)
adult كبير/كبيرة *kibeer/kibeera*
advance مقدم *mo'adam* (m)
» in advance مقدما *mo'adaman*
advertisement اعلان *e'laen* (m)
advertising دعاية *di'aiya* (f)
aeroplane طيارة *Taiyaara* (f)
after بعد *ba'd*
» afterwards بعدين *ba'dayn*

afternoon بعد الظهر *ba'd iDDohr*
» afternoon performance ماتيني *matinay*
aftershave كولونيا لبعد الحلاقة *kolonya liba'd il Hila'a* (f)
again كمان *kamaen*
against ضد *Ded*
agency وكالة *wikaela* (f)
AIDS ايدز *aydz*
air الهواء *il hawa* (m)
» by air جوى *gawwi*
air mail بريد جوى *bareed gawwi*
air conditioning تكييف *takyeef* (m)
airport مطار *maTaar* (m)
aisle ممر *mamar* (m)
alarm انزار *inzaar* (m)
» alarm clock منبة *minabih* (m)
alcohol كحول *koHol* (m)
» alcoholic (person) خمورجي *khamorgi*
all كل *kol*
allergic to حساسية ضد *Hasasaya Ded*
to allow: he/she allows يسمح/تسمح *yesmaH/tesmaH*
allowed مسموح *masmooH* (m/f)

179

all right (OK) او كى owkay

also ايضا aiDan

always دائما daiman

ambulance اسعاف is²aef (m)

American امريكي/امريكية amreeki/ amreekaya

amount كمية kimaya (f)

anaesthetic (general) بنج عام bing ²aem (m); (local) بنج موضعى bing mowDe²y (m)

and و wi

angry غضبان/غضبانة ghaDbaan/ ghaDbaana

animal حيوان Haiyawaen (m/f)

antibiotics مضادات حيوية mowDadaat Haiyawaya (f)

antique انتيكة anteeka

any اى ay

anyone اى شخص ay shakhS

anything اى حاجة ay Haga
» **anything else** حاجة تانية Haga tanya

anywhere اى مكان ay makaen

apartment شقة sha²a (f)

appendicitis مصران اعور moSraan a²war (m)

appetite نفس nifs (m)

apple تفاحة tofaHa (f)

to apply: he/she applies يتقدم/تتقدم yatqadam/tatqadam

appointment ميعاد mi²aed (m)

approximately تقريبا ta'reeban

arch قوس qoos (m)

architect مهندس معمارى/ مهندسة معمارية mohandis me²maeri (m)/mohandissa me²maeraya (f)

area منطقة manTe'a (f)

arm ذراع dera² (m)

armbands (swimming) عوامة اطفال ²awaemit aTfaal (f)

army جيش gaesh (m)

to arrange: he/she arranges يحضر/تحضر yeHDar/teHDar

arrest: under arrest مقبوض علية/عليها ma'booD ²alih/²aliha

arrival وصول woSool (m)

to arrive: he/she arrives وصل/وصلت waSal/waSalit

art فن fann (m)
» **art gallery** معرض فنون ma²araD finoon (m)

arthritis التهاب المفاصل iltihaeb il ilmafaaSil (m)

artificial صناعى Sina²ai

artist فنان/فنانة fanaen (m)/fanaena (f)

as (like) زى zay

as far as I know على حسب علمى ²ala Hasab ²ilmi

ashtray طفاية Taffaiya (f)

aspirin اسبرين asbireen (m)

asthma ربو raboo (m)

at once حالا Haelan

at (the) فى fi

attendant (bathing) عامل انقاذ ²amil inqaaz (m)

attractive جذاب/جذابة gazaeb/ gazaeba

aunt (father's sister) عمة ²amma (f) (mother's sister) خالة khaela (f)

author مؤلف/مؤلفة mo'aelif (m)/ mo'aelifa (f)

automatic اوتوماتيك otomatik

to avoid: he/she avoids يتجنب/تتجنب yataganab/tataganab

B

baby بيبى baybi (m)
» **baby food** اكل البيبى akl il baybi (m)
» **baby wipes** مساحات البيبى masaHaet il baybi (f/pl)

babysitter جليسة اطفال *galeesit aTfaal*

back (reverse side) ظهر *Dahr*

backwards للخلف *lil khalf*

bad (reverse side) وحش/وحشة *weHesh/weHsha*

bag شنطة *shanTa* (f)

bakery خباز *khabaez* (m)

balcony (theatre etc.) بلكون *balakown* (m)

bald اصلع *aSl³a*

ball كرة *kora* (f)

ballet بالية *ballay* (m)

balloon باللونة *balowna* (f)

bank بنك *bank* (m)

banknote بنكنوت *banknowt* (m)

bar بار *bar*; (chocolate) صباع شوكولاتة *Soba³ shokolaata* (m)

barber's حلاق *halae'* (m)

bargain لقطة *lo'Ta* (f)

basement بدرون *badrown* (m)

basin (bowl) حوض *HowD* (m)

basket سبت *sabat* (m)

bath بانيو *banyo* (m)

to have a bath: he/she has a bath ياخد/تاخد حمام *yakhod/takhod Hammaem*

bathroom حمام *Hammaem* (m)

battery بطارية *baTarayya* (f)

bay خليج *khaleeg* (m)

to be: he/she is يكون/تكون *yikoon/tikoon*

beach شاطىء *shaaTi'* (m)

beard ذقن *da'n* (m)

beautiful جميل/جميلة *gameel/gameela*

beauty جمال *gamael* (m)

because علشان *³alashaen*

bed سرير *sereer* (m)

bedroom غرفة نوم *ghorfit nowm* (f)

bee نحلة *naHla* (f)

beer بيرة *beera* (f)

before قبل *abl*

to begin يبدا/تبدا *yebda'/tebda'*;
 » it begins at 8pm
 يبدا الساعة ثمانية مساء *yebda issa³a tamanya masa'an*

beginner مبتدىء/مبتدئة *mobtadi' (m)/mobtadi'a* (f)

behind خلف *khalf*

to believe: he/she believes يؤمن/تؤمن *yo'min/to'min*

bell جرس *garas* (m)

below تحت *taHt*

belt حزام *Hizaem* (m)

bend منحنى *monHana* (m)

best الأحسن *il aHsan*

better احسن *aHsan*

between بين *bayn*

bicycle عجلة *³agala* (f)

bidet بيدية *beeday* (f)

big كبير/كبيرة *kibeer/kibeera*

bigger اكبر *akbar*

bill فاتورة *fatoora* (f)

bin زبالة *zibaela* (f)
 » bin liner كيس زبالة *kees zibaela* (m)

bird عصفورة *³aSfoora* (f)

birthday عيد ميلاد *³eed milaed* (m)

biscuit بسكوتة *baskowta* (f)

a bit شوية *showaiya*

to bite: he/she bites يعض/تعض *ye³oD/te³oD*

bitter مر *morr*

black اسود *eswid*
 » black and white (film)
 فيلم ابيض و اسود *film abyaD wi eswid*
 » black coffee قهوة سادة *'ahwa saeda*

blanket بطانية *baTanayya* (f)

bleach بوطاس *boTas* (m)

to bleed: he/she bleeds ينزف/تنزف *yenzif/tenzif*

blind اعمى/عمياء *a³ma (m)/³amya* (f)

blister كيس مايه *kees maiya* (m)

blonde شعر ذهبى *sha*ʰr dahabi

blood دم *dam* (m)

blue ازرق *azra'*

to board: he/she boards يركب/تركب
yerkab/terkab

boarding card بطاقة صعود *biTa'it*
*So*ʰ*ood* (f)

boat مركب *markib* (f)

» boat trip رحلة على مركب *reHla* ʰ*ala*
markib (f)

body جسم *gesm* (m)

to boil: he/she boils يسلق/تسلق
yeslo'/teslo'

boiled egg بيضة مسلوقة *bayDa*
masloo'a

boiler سخان *sakhaen* (m)

bone عظمة *ʰaDma* (f)

book كتاب *kitaeb* (m)

to book: he/she books يحجز/تحجز
yeHgiz/teHgiz

booking حجز *Hagz*

» booking office مكتب الحجز *maktab*
il Hagz

booklet كتيب *kotaiyib* (m)

bookshop مكتبة *maktaba* (f)

border (frontier) حدود *Hodood* (m)

boring ممل *momil* (m)/*momila* (f)

both هما الاثنين *homa il itnayn*

bottle ازازة *izaeza* (f)

bottle opener فتاحة *fataeHa* (f)

bowl طبق غويط *Taba' ghaweeT* (m)

box علبة *ʰelba* (f); (theatre) لوج
lowj (m)

box office مكتب التذاكر *maktab*
ittazaekir (m)

boy ولد *walad* (m)

boyfriend صديق *Sadeeq* (m)

bra سوتيان *sootyaen* (m)

bracelet غويشة *ghowaesha* (f)

brake فرملة *farmala* (f)

brand ماركة *marka* (f)

bread عيش *ʰaysh* (m)

to break : he/she breaks يكسر/تكسر
yikassar/tikassar

to break down: it has broken down
بايظة/بايظ *baiyiZ/baiyZa*

breakfast افطار *fiTaar* (m)

to breathe: he/she breathes
يتنفس/تتنفس *yetnafis/tetnafis*

bride عروسة *ʰaroosa* (f)

bridegroom عريس *ʰarees* (m)

bridge كوبرى *kobri* (m)

briefcase شنطة *shanTa* (f)

bright (colour) يلمع/تلمع
biyelmʰa(m)/*bitelmʰa* (f); (light)
فاتح *faetiH*

to bring: he/she brings يجيب/تجيب
yegeeb/tegeeb

British بريطانى/بريطانية *briTaani* (m)/
briTanaya (f)

broken مكسور/مكسورة *maksoor* (m)/
maksoora (f)

bronchitis التهاب رئوى *iltihaeb*
re'awi (m)

bronze برونز *bronz*

brown بنى *bonni*

bruise كدمة *kadma* (f)

brush فرشة *forsha* (f)

buffet بوفية *boofay* (f)

to build: he/she builds يبنى/تبنى
yebni/tebni

building بناء *bona* (m)

bulb (light) لمبة *lamba* (f)

bumper (car) اكصدام *ikSidaam* (m)

burn حرق *Har'* (m)

to burn: he/she burns يحرق/تحرق
yeHra'/teHra'

burnt محروق *maHroo'*

bus اوتوبيس *otobees* (m)

» by bus بالاوتوبيس *bil otobees*

business اعمال *aʰmael* (m/pl)

» business trip رحلة اعمال *reHlit*
aʰmael (f)

» **on business** فى مامورية *fi ma'mooraya*

businessman/woman رجل/سيدة اعمال *ragil* (m)/*saiyedat* (f) *a*ªmael

bus station موقف اوتوبيس *maw'aef otobees* (m)

bus stop محطة اوتوبيس *maHaTit otobees* (m)

busy مشغول/مشغولة *mashghool* (m)/ *mashghoola* (f)

but لكن *laekin*

butane gas بوتاجاز *botagaez* (m)

button زرار *zoorar* (m)

to buy: he/she buys يشترى/تشترى *yishteri/teshteri*

by (next to) بجانب *bigaenib*

C

cabin كابينة *kabeena* (f)

café قهوة *'ahwa* (f)

cake كيكة *kayka* (f)

to call (phone) مكالمة *mokalma* (f)

to call: he/she calls ينادى/تنادى *yinaedi/ tinaedi*

to be called: he/she is called اسمه/اسمها *ismoo/ismaha*

calm هادى ء/هادية *haedi* (m)/*hadya* (f)

camcorder كاميرة فيديو *kamerit vidyo* (f)

camera كاميرا *kamera* (f)

to camp: he/she camps يعسكر/تعسكر *ye*ªaskar/te*ª*askar*

camp bed سرير خيمة *sereer khayma*

camping gas وابور جاز *waboor gaez*

camping عسكر *ªaskar* (m)

campsite معسكر *mow*ªaskar* (m)

can: he/she can (to be able) يقدر/تقدر *ye'dar/te'dar*

can (tin) معلب *mo*ªalab* (m)

can opener فتاحة *fataeHa* (f)

to cancel: he/she cancels يلغى/تلغى *yelghi/telghi*

cancer سرطان *saraTaan* (m)

candle شمعة *sham*ªa* (f)

canoe قارب *'aerib* (m)

capital (city) عاصمة *ªaSima* (f)

car عربية *ªarabaya* (f)

» **by car** بالعربية *bil*ªarabaya*

» **car hire** عربيات للإيجار *ªarabiyaet lil iygar*

carafe شفشق *shafsha'* (m)

careful حريص/حريصة *HareeS* (m)/ *HareeSa* (f)

car park موقف عربيات *maw'af* *ªarabiyaet* (m)

carriage (train) عربية *ªarabaya* (f)

carrier bag شنطة المشتروات *shanTit il mooshtarawaat* (f)

to carry: he/she carries يشيل/تشيل *yesheel/tesheel*

carton كرتونة *kartowna* (f)

car wash غسيل سيارات *ghaseel saiyaraat* (m)

cash كاش *kash* (m)

to pay cash: he/she pays cash يدفع/تدفع كاش *yedfa*ª/tedfa*ª kash*

cash desk الخزينة *il khazeena* (f)

cashpoint ماكينة سحب الفلوس *makinaet saHb il filoos* (f)

castle قلعة *'al*ªa* (f)

cat قطة *oTa* (f)

to catch: he/she catches يمسك/تمسك *yemsik/temsik*

cathedral كاتدرائية *katedra'aya* (f)

Catholic كاثوليكى *katowleeki*

CD سى دى *seedee* (m)

CD-Rom سى دى روم *seedee rom* (m)

centimetre سنتيمتر *santimeeter* (m)

central مركزى/مركزية *markazi/ markazaya*

central heating تدفئة مركزية *tadfe'a markazaya* (f)

centre مركز *markaz* (m)

century قرن *qarn* (m)

CEO (chief executive officer) رئيس مجلس الادارة ra'ees maglis il idaara (m)

certificate شهادة shahaeda (f)

chain سلسلة silsila (f)

chair كرسي korsi (m)

chair lift كرسي مصعد korsi maSaad (m)

chalet شالية shalay (m)

champagne شامبانيا shambanya (f)

championship بطولة boToola (f)

change (coins) فكة fakka (f)

to change: he/she changes يغير/تغير yeghaiyar/teghaiyar

changing room غرفة تغيير الملابس ghorfit taghyeer il malaebis (f)

chapel كنيسة kineesa (f)

charge (money) ثمن taman (m)

cheap رخيص/رخيصة rakheeS (m)/ rakheeSa (f)

checked (pattern) كاروه karo (m)

check-in (desk) مكتب التسجيل maktab ittazgeel (m)

to check-in: he/she checks in يسجل/تسجل yesagil/tesagil

checkout (till) خزينة khazeena (f)

Cheers! في صحتك/صحتك/صحتكم fi SeHetak (m)/fi SeHetik (f)/fi SeHetkom (pl)

chest صدر Sedr (m)

chewing gum لبان libaen (m)

chicken فرخة farkha (f)

chicken pox جديري godaeri (m)

child طفل Tefl (m)

children اطفال aTfaal (pl)

china صيني Seenee (m)

chips شيبس shibs (m)

chocolate(s) شوكولاتة shokolaata (f)

to choose: he/she chooses يختار/تختار yekhtaar/tekhtaar

Christian مسيحي/مسيحية meseeHi(m)/meseeHaya (f)

» Christian name الاسم الاول il 'ism il awil

Christmas الكريسماس il krismas (m)

» Christmas Day يوم الكريسماس yowm il krismas

» Christmas Eve ليلة الكريسماس laylit il krismas

church كنيسة kineesa (f)

cigar سيجار sigaar (m)

cigarette سيجارة sigaara (f)

cinema سينما sinema (f)

circle دائرة daira (f); (in theatre) بلكون balakown (m)

circus سيرك serk (m)

city مدينة madeena (f)

class فصل faSl (m)

classical كلاسيكي/كلاسيكاية klaseeki/ klaseekaya

classical music موسيقى كلاسيكية mowseeka klaseekaya

to clean: he/she cleans ينظف/تنظف yenaDaf/tenaDaf

clean نظيف/نظيفة neDeef/neDeefa

clever شاطر/شاطرة shaaTir/shaTra

cliff منحدر monHadar (m)

climate الجو il gaw (m)

to climb: he/she climbs يتسلق/تتسلق yetsala'/tetsala'

clinic عيادة ªiyaeda (f)

cloakroom حجرة المعاطف Hogrit il maªaTif (f)

clock ساعة saªa (f)

close (by) قريب oraiyib

to close: he/she closes يقفل/تقفل ye'fil/te'fil

closed مقفول/مقفولة ma'fool/ ma'foola

clothes ملابس malaebis (pl)

cloudy مغيم meghaiyim

club نادي naedi (m)

clutch (car) دبرياج debriyaj (m)

coach اوتوبيس otobees (m)

coast ساحل saeHil (m)

coat بالطو balToo (m)

coat-hanger شماعة shamae'a (f)

cocktail كوكتيل koktayl (m)

coffee قهوة 'ahwa (f)

coin قرش 'ersh (m)

cold (adj.) بارد/باردة baerid/barda

to have a cold: he/she has a cold
عنده/عندها برد 'andoo/'andaha bard

collar ياقة ya'a (m)

colleague زميل/زميلة zameel (m)/
zameela (f)

college كلية kollaya (f)

colour لون lown (m)

colour-blind عنده/عندها عمى الوان
'andoo/'andaha 'ama alwaen

comb مشط meshT (m)

to come: he/she comes جاى/جاية
gaiy/gaiia

to come back: he/she comes back
يرجع/ترجع yerga'/terga'

to come in: he/she comes in
يدخل/تدخل yedkhol/tedkhol

come in! أدخل! edkhol

comedy كوميديا komedya (m)

comfortable مريح/مريحة moreeH/
moreeHa

comic (magazine) مجلة كوميدية
migalla komidaya (f)

commercial تجارى/تجارية toogaeri
(m)/toogaraya (f)

common (usual) معتاد mo'ataed;
(shared) مشترك/مشتركة moshtarak/
moshtaraka

الشيوعية
ish sheeyoo'aya (f)
communism

commission عمولة 'omoola (f)

company شركة sherka (f)

compared with ... بالمقارنة ب
bilmoqarna bi...

compartment ديوان diwaen (m)

to complain: he/she complains يشتكى/
تشتكى yeshteki/teshteki

» complaint شكوة shakwa (f)

complete كامل/كاملة kaemil (m)/
kamla (f)

complicated معقد/معقدة mo'aqed
(m)/mo'aqada (f)

compulsory اجبارى/اجبارية igbaeri
(m)/igbaraya (f)

composer مؤلف موسيقى mow'alif
mowsiqa (m)

computer كومبيوتر kompyootar (m)

concert حفلة موسيقية Hafla
mosiqaya (f)

concert hall قاعة موسيقية qa'a
mosiqaya (f)

concession تخفيض خاص takhfeeD
khaS (m)

concussion ارتجاج فى المخ irtigaeg
fil mokh (m)

condition حالة Hala (f)

condom كبوت kaboot (m)

connection مواصلة mowaSla (f)

conference مؤتمر mo'tamar (m)

to confirm: he/she confirms يؤكد/تؤكد
yow'akid/tow'akid

il المحافظة على البيئة
moHafZa 'ala il bee'a (f)
conservation

conservative محافظ moHaafiZ (m)

constipation امساك imsaek (m)

consulate قنصلية onSolaya (f)

contact lens عدسات لاصقة 'adasaet
laSqa (f/pl)

» contact lens cleaner
منظف العدسات اللاصقة monaZaf il
'adasaet ilaSqa (m)

contagious معدى/معدية mo'di (m)/
mo'daya (f)

continent قارة qara (f)

contraceptive مانع للحمل mane' lil
Haml (m)

control (passport) تسجيل tasgeel (m)

to continue: he/she continues
يكمل/تكمل yekamil/tekamil

convenient ملائمة/ملائم mola'im
(m)/mola'ma (f)

to cook: he/she cooks يطبخ/تطبخ
yeTbokh/teTbokh

cooked مطبوخ maTbookh

cooker فرن forn (m)

cool بارد/باردة baerid/barda

cool box علبة ثلج ᵉelbit talg (f)

copy نسخة noskha (f)

corkscrew فتاحة ازايز fataeHit
'azayiz (f)

corner (outside) ركنة rokna (f)

correct صحيح/صحيحة SaHeeH (m)/
SaHeeHa (f)

corridor ممر mamar (m)

cosmetics منتجات تجميل montagaet
tagmeel (m/pl)

to cost: it costs ثمنها tamano/tamanha

cot سرير اطفال sereer aTfaal (m)

cotton (material) نبات القطن nabaet il
'oTn (m); (thread) خيط قطن khayT
'oTn (m)

cotton wool قطنة oTna (f)

cough كحة koHa (f)

to cough: he/she coughs يكح/ تكح
yekoH/tekoH

to count: he/she counts يعد/تعد
yaᵉid/taᵉid

counter (post office) مكتب البيع
maktab il biyᵉa (m)

country دولة dawla (f)
» in the country فى الريف fi irreef

countryside الريف irreef (m)

couple (pair) جوز gowz (m)

course (lessons) كورس kors (m)

court (law) محكمة maHkama (f)
(tennis) ملعب malᵉab (m)

cover (lid) غطاء ghaTa (f)

cow بقرة baᵉra (f)

crab كابوريا kaborya (f)

cramp شد عضلى shad ᵉaDali (m)

cream (food) قشطة ishTa (f);
(lotion) كريم kraym (m); (colour) كريم
kraym (m)

credit card كارت ائتمان kart
i'timaen (m)

cricket كريكت kriket (m)

crisps شيبسى shibsi (m)

cross (Christian) صليب Saleeb (m)

to cross: he/she crosses يعدى/ تعدى
yeᵉadi/teᵉadi

cross-country اختراق الضاحية ikhtera'
iDDaHya (m)

crossing عبور ᵉoboor (m)

crossroad مفترق الطرق moftaraq
iTToro' (m)

crowd زحام ZiHam (m)

crowded مزحوم mazHoom (m)

crown تاج taeg (m)

cruise رحلة بحرية reHla baHaraya (f)

crutch عكاز ᵉokaez (m)

to cry: he/she cries يبكى/تبكى
yebki/tebki

crystal كريستال kristael (m)

cup فنجان fingaen (m)

cupboard دولاب doolaeb (m)

cure علاج ᵉilaeg (m)

to cure: he/she cures يشفى/تشفى
yeshfi/teshfi

curly مموج momawig

curry كارى kaeri (m)

current (electricity) تيار taiyaar (m)

curtain ستارة sitara (f)

curve منحنى monHana (m)

cushion مخدة makhadda (f)

customs جمرك gomrok (m)

customer زبون ziboon (m)

to cut: he/she cuts يقطع/تقطع
yeᵉTaᵉ/teᵉTaᵉ

to cut oneself: he/she cut himself/
herself اتعور/اتعورت
itᵉawar/itᵉawarit

cycling ركوب العجل rokoob il ªagal

cyclist راكب العجلة raekib il ªagala(m)

D

daily يوميا yowmayan

dairy products منتجات الألبان montageat albaen (pl)

damage ضرر Darar (m)

damp مبلول/مبلولة mablool/mabloola

dance رقص ra'S (m)

to dance: he/she dances يرقص/ترقص yor'oS/tor'oS

danger خطر khaTar (m)

dangerous خطير/خطيرة khaTeer (m)/ khaTeera (f)

dark (colour) غامق/غامقة ghaemi'/ gham'a; (light) ضلمه Dalma

darling حبيبى/حبيبتى Habeebee (m)/ Habibti (f)

date (day) تاريخ tareekh (m); (fruit) بلح balaH (m)

daughter ابنة ibna (f)

daughter-in-law زوجة الابن zowgit il ibn (f)

day يوم yowm (m)
» day after tomorrow بعد بكرة bªad bokra
» day before yesterday اول امبارح awil imbareH

dead ميت/ميتة maiyit/maiyita

dead end منتهى الطريق montaha iTTaree'

deaf اطرش/طرشة aTrash/Tarsha

dear (loved) عزيزى/عزيزتي ªazeezi/ªazeezaeti; (expensive) غالي/غالية ghaeli/ghalya

death موت mowt (m)

debt دين dayn (m)

decaffeinated coffee قهوة بدون كافيين 'ahwa bidoon kafyeen (f)

deck سطح المركب saTH il markib (m)

to decide: he/she decides يقرر/تقرر yeqarar/teqarar

to declare: he/she declares يعلن/تعلن yoªlin/toªlin

deep عميق/عميقة ªameeq/ªameeqa

deer غزال ghazael (m)

defect عيب ªayb

defective بايظ/بايظة baiyiZ/baiyZa

definitely بالتأكيد bitta'keed

degree (temperature, university) درجة daraga (f)

delay تأخير ta'kheer (m)

delicate رقيق/رقيقة ra'ee'/ra'ee'a

delicious لذيذ/لذيذة lazeez/lazeeza

delighted مبسوط/مبسوطة mabsooT/ mabsooTa

to deliver: he/she delivers وصل/وصلت waSal/waSalit

delivery توصيل tawSeel (m)

demonstration مظاهرة moZahra (f)

dentist دكتور/دكتورة سنان doktowr (m)/doktowrit (f) sinaen

dentures سنان صناعية sinaen Sinaªeya (pl)

deodorant مزيل لرائحة العرق mozeel li ra'iHit il ªara' (m)

to depart: he/she departs يسافر/تسافر yisaefir/tisaefir

department (in shop) قسم qesm (m)

department store محل maHal (m)

departure سفر safar (m)

departure lounge قاعة السفر qaªit issafar (f)

deposit وديعة wadeeªa (f)

depth عمق ªomq (m)

desert صحراء SaHara' (f)

to describe: he/she describes يوصف/توصف yowSif/towSif

description وصف waSf (m)

design تصميم taSmeem (m)

designer مصمم/مصممة *moSamim* (m)/*moSamima* (f)

dessert حلو *Helw* (m)

destination جهة السفر *gehit issafar* (f)

detergent صابون الغسيل *Saboon il ghaseel* (m)

to develop: he/she develops يطور/تطور *yeTawar/teTawar*

diabetes سكر *sokkar*

to dial: he/she dials يطلب/تطلب *yoTlob/toTlob*

dialling code رقم الكود *raqam il kowd* (m)

dialling tone الحرارة *il Haraara* (f)

diamond ماسة *maesa* (f)

diarrhoea اسهال *is-hael* (m)

dice زهر *zahr* (pl)

dictionary قاموس *qamoos* (m)

to die: he/she dies يموت/تموت *yemoot/temoot*

died مات/ماتت *maet/maetit*

diesel ديزل *deezil* (m)

diet رجيم *rejeem* (m)

different(ly) مختلف/مختلفة *mokhtalif/mokhtalifa*

difficult صعب *Sa°b*

digital رقمي *raqami*

digital camera كاميرا ديجيتال *kamera dijeetal*

dinghy قارب مطاط *'aerib maTaaT* (m)

dining room اودة السفرة *owdit issofra* (f)

dinner عشاء *°asha* (f)

dinner jacket جاكت سواري *jaket sowaray*

diplomat دبلوماسي/دبلوماسية *diblomaesi* (m)/*diblomaesaya* (f)

direct (train) مباشر *mobaeshir*

direction اتجاه *itigah* (m)

directory دليل *daleel* (m)

dirty قذر/قذرة *qazir* (m)/*qazira* (f)

disabled معوق/معوقة *mo°awaq* (m)/*mo°awaqa* (f)

disappointment خيبة الامل *khaebit il amal* (m)

disc (computer) ديسك *disk* (m)

disco ديسكو *diskow* (m)

discount تخفيض *takhfeeD* (m)

dish طبق *Taba'* (m)

dishwasher غسالة صحون *ghasaelit SoHoon* (f)

disinfectant مطهر *moTahir* (m)

dislocated مخلوع/مخلوعة *makhloo°* (m)/*makhloo°a* (f)

disposable مستهلك/مستهلكة *mostahlak/mostahlaka*

›› disposable camera
كاميرا للاستهلاك الفوري *kamera lil istihlaek il fawri* (f)

›› disposable nappies
بامبرز *bambers* (pl)

distance مسافة *masaefa* (f)

district ضاحية *DaHaya* (f)

to disturb: he/she disturbs يزعج/تزعج *yez°ig/tez°ig*

to dive: he/she dives يغوص/تغوص *yaghooS/taghooS*

diversion تحويلة *taHweela* (f)

diving غوص *ghowS* (m)

diving board منصة غطس *minaSit ghaTs* (f)

divorced مطلق/مطلقة *moTalaq* (m)/*moTalaqa* (f)

DIY محل اخدم نفسك *maHal ikhdim nafsak* (m)

dizzy دايخ/دايخة *daiyikh/daiykha*

to do: he/she does بيعمل/بتعمل *biye°amil/bite°amil*

doctor دكتور/دكتورة *doktowr* (m)/*doktowra* (f)

documents مستندات *mostanadaet* (f/pl)

dog كلب/كلبة *kalb* (m)/*kalba* (f)

doll عروسة *°aroosa* (f)

dollar دولار *dollaar* (m)

dome قبة *'oba* (f)

donkey حمار/حمارة *Homaar* (m)/
Homaara (f)

door باب *baeb* (m)

double دوبل *dobl*

double bed سرير مذدوج *sereer
mozdawag* (m)

down تحت *taHt*

download تنزيل *tanzeel* (m)

downstairs الدور اللى تحت *iddowr
ili taHt*

drains مجارى *magaeri* (m)

draught beer بيرة من البرميل *beera
min il barmeel* (f)

to draw: he/she draws (picture)
يرسم/ترسم *yersim/tersim*

drawing رسم *rasm* (m)

dreadful سىء/سيئة *saiyi'* (m)/
saiyi' a (f)

dress فستان *foostaen* (m)

to dress: he/she gets dressed
يلبس/تلبس *yelbis/telbis*

dressing (medical) غيار طبى *ghiyaar
Tebi* (m); (salad) صوص *SowS* (m)

drink مشروب *mashroob* (m)

to drink: he/she drinks يشرب/تشرب
yishrab/tishrab

drinking (water) مياة صالحة للشرب
miyah SaliHa lil shorb (f)

to drive: he/she drives يسوق/تسوق
yesoo'/tesoo'

driving licence رخصة قيادة *rokhSit
qiyaeda* (f)

drowsiness نعاس *noa°aes* (m)

drug دواء *dawa* (f)

» drug addict مدمن/مدمنة مخدرات
modmin (m)/*modmina* (f) *mokhadaraat*

dry ناشف/ناشفة *naeshif/nashfa*;
(wine) نبيت دراى *nebeet dry*

dry-cleaner's مغسلة على الناشف
maghsaela °ala innaeshif (f)

dubbed دوبلاج *doblaj*

dummy (baby's) بزازة *bazaeza* (f)

during خلال *khilael*

dust تراب *toraab* (m)

dustbin صفيحة زبالة *SafeeHit zibaela* (f)

dusty مترب/متربة *motrib/motriba*

duty (tax) ضريبة *Dareeba* (f)

duty-free معفية من الضرائب *ma°faya
min iDDaraiyib* (f)

duvet لحاف *liHaef* (m)

DVD دى فى دى *deeveedee* (f)

» DVD player جهاز دى فى دى *gihaez
deeveedee*

each كل *kol*

ear infection إلتهاب فى الأذن *iltihaeb
fil wedn* (m)

early بدرى *badri*

to earn: he/she earns يكسب/تكسب
yiksab/tiksab

earring حلق *Hala'* (m)

earth الأرض *il arD* (f)

east شرق *shar'* (m)

» eastern شرقى/شرقية *shar' i/shar'aya*

Easter عيد القيامة *°eed il qiyaema* (m)

easy سهل *sahl*

to eat: he/she eats اكل/تاكل *yaekol/
taekol*

economy الاقتصاد *il iqtiSaad* (m)

edible قابل للاكل *qaabil lil akl*

effort مجهود *mag hood* (m)

egg بيضة *bayDa* (f)

» eggs بيض *bayD* (pl)

either... or... او...اما... *imma... aw...*

election انتخابات *intikhabaet* (pl)

electrician كهربائى/كهربائية *kahrobae'i*
(m)/*kahrobae'aya* (f)

electricity كهرباء *kahrabba* (f)

electronic الكترونى/الكترونية
elektrowni/elektrownaya

email ايميل *eemayl* (m)

to email: he/she sends an email
يبعث/تبعث اي مايل *yeb*at/teb*at
eemayl*

to embark: he/she embarks (on boat)
يركب /تركب *yerkab/terkab*

embarrassing مخجلة/مخجل *mokhgil/
mokhgila*

embassy سفارة *sifaara* (f)

emergency طوارىء *Tawaari'* (pl)

empty فاضي/فاضية *faaDi/faDya*

end نهاية *nihaya* (f)

to end: he/she ends ينهى /تنهى
yenhi/tenhi

energy طاقة *Taaqa* (f)

engaged (to be married)
مخطوب/مخطوبة *makhToob/
makhTooba*; (occupied) مشغول
مشغولة *mashghool/mashghoola*

England انجلترا *ingilterra* (f)

English انجليزي/انجليزية *ingleezi/
ingleezaya*

to enjoy: he/she enjoys يستمتع /تستمتع
*yastemte*a/tastemte*a*

enough كفاية *kifaya*

to enter: he/she enters يدخل /تدخل
yedkhol/tedkhol

entertainment ترفيه *tarfeeh* (m)

entrance مدخل *madkhal* (m)

envelope مظروف *maZroof* (m)

environment بيئة *bee'a* (f)

environmentally friendly
صديق للبيئة/صديقة للبيئة *Sadeeq
(m)/Sadeeqit (f) il bee'a*

epilepsy صرع *Sara*a* (m)

epileptic عندة/عندها صرع *andoo
(m)/*andaha (f) Sara*a*

equal متساوي/متساوية *motasaewi/
motasaewia*

equipment اجهزة *aghiza* (pl)

escalator سلالم متحركة *salaelim
motaHarika* (pl)

especially خاصة *khaSa*

essential مهم/مهمة *mohim/mohima*

estate agent سمسار/سمسارة عقارات
*simsaar (m)/simsaarit (f) *iqaraat*

even (including) حتى *Hatta*

even number ارقام متساوي
arqam motasaewia (f)

evening مساء *masa'*

every كل *kol*

everyone كل واحد/واحدة *kol waHid
(m)/waHida* (f)

everything كل شىء *kol shai'*

everywhere كل مكان *kol makaen*

exact(ly) بالضبط *biZZabT*

examination امتحان *imtiHan* (m)

exams أمتحانات *imtiHanaet* (pl)

example مثل *masal* (m)

for example مثلا *masalan*

excellent ممتاز/ممتازة *momtaez/
momtaeza*

except ما عدا *ma*ada*

excess baggage زيادة فى الوزن
ziyaeda fil wazn (f)

to exchange: he/she exchanges
يتبادل/تتبادل *yatabaedal/tatabaedal;
(money) يغير عملة/تغير عملة *yeghaiyar/
teghaiyar *omla*

exchange rate سعر تغيير العملة *se*r
taghyeer il *omla* (m)

excited ثائر/ثائرة *thaei'r/thaei'ra*

exciting مثير/مثيرة *motheer/
motheera*

excursion رحلة *reHla* (f)

excuse me بعد اذنك *ba*d iznak* (to
m)/iznik (to f)

executive تنفيذي/تنفيذية *tanfeezi (m)/
tanfeezaya* (f)

exercise تدريب *tadreeb* (m)

exhibition معرض *ma*raD* (m)

exit خروج *khoroog* (m)

to expect: he/she expects يتوقع /تتوقع
*yatawaqa*a/tatawaqa*a*

expensive غالي/غالية ghaeli/ghalya

experience خبرة khebra (f)

experiment تجربة tagroba (f)

expert (person) خبير/خبيرة khabeer (m)/khabeera (f)

to explain: he/she explains
يشرح/تشرح yeshraH/teshraH

explosion تفجير tafgeer (m)

export تصدير taSdeer (m)

to export: he/she exports يصدر/تصدر
yeSaddar/teSaddar

express اكسبريس eksebrays

extension cable امتداد كابل imtidaed kaebil (m)

external خارجي/خارجية khaerigi/khaerigaya

extra إضافي/إضافيه iDaafi/iDaafaya

to extract: he/she extracts
يستخرج/تستخرج yestakhrig/testakhrig

eyelash رمش العين rimsh il ªayan (m)

eyeliner قلم عيون alam ªeyoon (m)

eyeshadow ظل عيون Zil ªeyoon (m)

F

fabric قماش omaesh (m)

facilities تسهيلات tas-heelaet (pl)

fact واقع waqeª (m)
» in fact في الواقع fil waqeª

factory مصنع maSnaª (m)

to fail: he/she fails (exam/text)
يسقط/تسقط yes'aT/tes'aT

failure فشل fashal (m)

to faint: he/she faints عليه/عليها أغمى
oghma ªalay/ªalayha

fair (haired) شعر اصفر shaªr aSfar (m);
(just) عادل/عادلة ªadil/ªadila

faith ايمان eemaen (m)

fake مزور/مزورة mozawar/mozawara

to fall: he/she falls يقع/تقع yo'aª/to'aª

false غير صحيح ghayr SaHeeH

familiar معروف/معروفة maªroof/maªroofa

family عائلة ªayla (f)

famous مشهور/مشهورة mashhoor/mashhoora

fan (air) مروحة marwaHa (f);
(supporter) مشجع/مشجعة moshagiª/moshagiªa

fantastic هايل/هايلة haeyil/haeyla,
عظيم/عظيمة ªazeem (m)/ªazeema (f)

far (away) بعيد/بعيدة beªeed/beªeeda

fare اجرة ogra (f)

farm مزرعة mazraªa (f)

farmer مزارع mozaereª (m)

fashion(able) موضة mowda (f)

fast سريع/سريعة sareeª/sareeªa

fat تخين/تخينة tekheen/tekheena

fatal مميت/مميتة momeet/momeeta

father اب ab (m)

father-in-law حماة Hama (m)

fault عيب ªayb (m)

faulty بايظ/بايظة baiyiZ/baiyiZa

favourite مفضل/مفضلة mofaDal/mofaDala
» favourite film فيلمي المفضل filmi il mofaDal (m)

fax فاكس faks (m)

feather ريشة reesha (f)

fed up (bored) زهق/زهقت zehi'/zeh'it

fee اجرة ogra (f)

to feed: he/she feeds يغزى / تغزى yeghazi/teghazi

to feel: he/she feels (emotion)
يشعر/تشعر yeshªor/teshªor

female انثى onsa (f)

feminist: he/she is a feminist
يناصر/تناصر حقوق المراة yenaSir/tenaSir Ho'oo' il mar'a

ferry معدية maªadaya (f)

festival مهرجان mahragaen (m)

F

to fetch: he/she fetches يجيب / تجيب yegeeb/tegeeb

fever حرارة Haraara (f)

(a) few بعض baªD

fiancé(e) خطيب/خطيبة khaTeeb (m)/khaTeeba (f)

fibre فيبر faiybar (m)

field غيط ghayT (m)

fig تين teen (m)

to fight: he/she fights يتخانق/تتخانق yetkhaeni'/tetkhaeni'

file (documents, computer) ملف malaf (m); (nail/DIY) مبرد mabrad (m)

to fill (up): he/she fills (up) يملىء تملى yemla/temla

filling (dental) حشو Hashw (m)

film فيلم film (m)

» film star نجم سينمائى/نجمة سينمائية negm sinemae'i(m) /negma sinemae'aya(f)

filter فلتر filter (m)

financial مالى maeli (m)

to find: he/she finds لقى/لقت la'a/la'it

fine (OK) تمام tamaem;(penalty) غرامة gharaama (f); (weather) (الجو il gaw gameel (m) جميل

finger صباع Sobaª (m)

to finish: he/she finishes يخلص/تخلص yekhallaS/tekhallaS

fire حريق Haree'a (f)

fire brigade المطافى il maTaafi (m)

fire extinguisher طفاية حريق Tafaiyit Haree' (f)

fireworks صواريخ Sawareekh (pl)

firm جامد gaemid/gamda (company) شركة shirka (f)

first اول/اولة awil/oola

» first aid اسعافات اولية isªafaet awilaya (pl)

» first aid kit عدة الاسعافات الاولية ªedit il isªafaet awilaya (f)

fish سمك samak (m)

to fish: he/she goes fishing يصطاد/تصطاد yeSTaad/teSTaad

fishing rod سنارة sinnaara (f)

to be fit: he/she is fit (healthy) عنده/عندها لياقة بدنية ªandoo/ ªandaha liyaqa badanaya

to fit: he/she fits (is suitable) يناسب/تناسب yinaesib/tinaesib

» that fits you well مقاسك بالظبط ma'aesak (to m)/ma'aesik (to f) bil ZabT

fitting room غرفة القياس ghorfit il qiyaes (f)

to fix: he/she fixes (mend) يصلح/تصلح yeSalaH/teSalaH

fizzy فوار fawaar/fawaara

flag علم ªalam (m)

flash (camera) فلاش filaesh (m)

flat (apartment) شقة sha'a (f)

flat (level) متساوى/متساوية motasaewi/motasawaya

flat battery البطارية فاضية il bataraya faDya (f)

flavour طعم Taªm (m)

flight رحلة جوية reHla gawaya (f)

flippers فليبرز fliberz (m)

floor بلاط balaaT (pl)

» on the first floor فى الدور الاول fiddowr il awil (m)

» ground floor الدور الارضى iddowr il arDi (m)

flour دقيق di'ee' (m)

flower وردة warda (f)

flu/influenza انفلونزا infloowenza (m)

fluent طليق/طليقة Talee'/Talee'a

fluid سائل sae'il (m)

fly دبانة debaena (f)

fly spray رشاش ضد الحشرات الطائرة rashaash Ded il Hasharaat il Ta'aera (m)

dictionary

192

to fly: he/she flies يطير/تطير yeTir/teTir

fog ضباب Dabaab (m)

foggy فى ضباب fi Dabaab

foil ورق الومنيوم wara' alomonyom (pl)

folk music موسيقى الفلكلور mooseeqa il folklowr (f)

to follow: he/she follows يتابع/تتابع yetaebe^a/tetaebe^a

following (next) اللاحق/الاحقه ilaHiq/ilaHiqa

food اكل akl (m)

food poisoning تسمم الاكل tasamom il akl (m)

foot قدم 'adam (m)

» on foot على الاقدام ^ala il aqdaem

football كرة القدم korit il 'adam (f)

for ل li

forbidden ممنوع mamnoo^a

foreign(er) اجنبى/اجنبية agnaebi/agnabaya

forest غابة ghaeba (f)

to forget: he/she forgets ينسى/تنسى yensa/tensa

to forgive: he/she forgives يسامح/تسامح yisaemiH/tisaemiH

fork شوكة showka (f)

form طلب Talab (m)

fortnight اسبوعين izboo^ayn

fortress حصن HeSn (m)

forward للامام lil amaem

forwarding address عنوان المرسل اليه ^enwaen il morsal ilayh (m)

foundation (make-up) ماكياج makiyaaj (m)

fountain نافورة nafoora (f)

fox ثعلب ta^lab (m)

foyer مدخل madkhal (m)

fracture كسر kasr (m)

fragile قابل للكسر 'abil lil kasr (m)

frankly بصراحة biSaraHa

free (available/unoccupied) فاضى/فاضية faaDi/faDya

free of charge ببلاش bibalaesh

freedom حرية Horayya (f)

to freeze: he/she freezes يثلج/تثلج yetalig/tetalig

freezer فريزر freezar (m)

French فرنسى/فرنسية faransaewi/faransawaya

French stick عيش فينو ^aysh finoo (m)

frequent كثيرا katheeran

fresh طازج Tazah

fridge الثلاجة ittalaega (f)

fried محمر/محمرة maHammar/maHammara

friend صديق/صديقة Sadeeq (m)/Sadeeqa (f)

frightened خائف/خائفة khaeyif/khayfa

frog ضفدعة Dofda^a (m)

from من min

front وجة/واجهة wagh/wagha

» in front of قدام oddaem

frontier الجبهة il gabha (f)

frozen مثلج/مثلجة metallig/metalliga

fruit فاكهة fak-ha (f)

to fry: he/she fries يحمر/تحمر yeHammar/teHammar

frying pan صانية تحمير Sanayit taHmeer (f)

fuel وقود woqood (pl)

full مليان/مليانة malyaen/malyaena

» full board بالاكل فول بورد bil akl fool bord

» full up كامل العدد kaemil il ^adad

to have fun: he/she has fun بينبسط/تتنبسط biyenbesiT/bitenbesiT

it was fun اخر انبساط aekhir inbisaaT

to function: he/she functions يعمل/تعمل ye^mil/te^mil

funeral جنازة ganaeza (f)

funfair ملاهى malaehi (f)

funny (amazing) مزهل/مزهلة mozhil/
mozhila; (entertaining) مسلي/مسلية
mosalli/mosallaya;
(peculiar) عجيب/عجيبة ªageeb/
ªageeba

fur فرو farw (m)

furniture عفش ªafsh (pl)

further on ابعد abªad

G

gallery معرض maªaraD (m)

gambling قمار 'omar (m)

game (match) ماتش mutch (m)

garage (for repairs) جاراج garaaj (m)
(for petrol) محطة بنزين maHaTit
benzeen (f)

garden جنينة ginayna (f)

garlic ثوم towm (m)

gas غاز ghaez (m)

» gas bottle/cylinder انبوبة بوتاجاز
amboobit botagaez (f)

gate بوابة bawaeba (f)

general عام ªaem

» in general عموما ªomooman

general practitioner, GP دكتور/دكتورة
doktowr (m)/doktowra (f)

generous كريم/كريمة kareem/
kareema

gentleman جنتلمان jentilmaen (m)

genuine اصيل/اصيلة aSeel/aSeela

German measles حصبة HaSba (f)

to get off: he/she gets off ينزل/تنزل
yenzil/tenzil

to get on: he/she gets on يركب/تركب
yerkab/terkab

gift هدية hedayya (f)

gin جن jin (m)

girl بنت bint (f)

girlfriend صديقة Sadeeqa (f)

to give: he/she gives يدى/تدى
yedi/tedi

he/she gives back يرجع/ترجع
yerageª/terageª

give way يفسح الطريق yefsaH
iTTaree'

glass كوبايا kobbaya (f)

glasses (spectacles) نضاره naDara (f)

gloves جوانتي gwanti (m)

glue صمغ Samgh (m)

gluten-free منتجات بدون شعير
montagaet bidoon sheªeer

to go: he/she goes يذهب/تذهب
yerooH/terooH

» he/she goes away (travels)
يسافر/تسافر yasaefir/tesaefir

» he/she goes down ينزل/تنزل
yenzil/tenzil

» he/she goes in يدخل/تدخل
yedkhol/tedkhol

» he/she goes out يخرج/تخرج
yekhrog/tekhrog

» let's go! يالا بينا yalla beena

goal جول gowl (m)

goat معزة maªza (f)

god الله allah

goggles نظارة غطس naDarit ghaTs (f)

gold ذهب dahab (m)

golf جولف golf (m)

» golf clubs مضارب الجولف maDarrib
il golf (pl)

» golf course ملعب الجولف malªab
il golf (m)

good كويس/كويسة kwayyis/kwayyissa

» good day اهلا و سهلا ahlan wa
sahlan

» good evening مساء الخير misa' il
kheer

» good morning صباح الخير SabaH
il kheer

» good night تصبح/تصبحى على خير
tiSbaH (to m)/tiSbaHi (to f) ªala
kheer

goodbye مع السلامة maªassalaema

government حكومة Hokooma (f)

grammar قواعد qawaʾid (m)

grandchildren الاحفاد il aHfaed (pl)

granddaughter حفيدتي Hafidti (f)

grandfather جد ged (m)

grandmother جدة geda (f)

grandparents الجدود il gedood (pl)

grandson حفيدي Hafeedi (m)

grass نجيلة negeela (f)

greasy دهني dehni

great! عظيم aZeem

green اخضر/خضراء akhDar/khaDra

greengrocer's خضري khoDari (m)

to greet: he/she greets يحي/تحي
yeHaiyi/teHaiyi

grey رمادي romaadi

grilled مشوي/مشوية mashwi/
mashwaya

grocer's بقالة biʾaela (f)

ground (sports) ارض الملعب arD il
malʾab

ground floor الدور الارضي iDDowr
il arDi (m)

group مجموعة magmooʾa (f)

guarantee ضمان Damaan (m)

guest زائر/زائرة zaʾir (m)/zaʾira (f)

guest house بنسيون bansyown (m)

guide (person) الدليل iddaleel (m)

» guided tour دورة بمرافقة الدليل
dawraat bimorfaqit iddeleel

guidebook دليل daleel (m)

guilty مذنب/مذنبة moznib/mozniba

guitar جيتار geetaar (m)

gun مسدس mosaddis

hair شعر shaʾr (pl)

hairbrush فرشة شعر forshit shaʾr (f)

haircut قصة شعر ʾaSit shaʾr (f)

hairdresser كوافير kwaffer (m)

hairdryer سشوار seshwar (m)

---

hairspray رشاش للشعر rashaash il
shaʾr (m)

half نصف noS

half an hour نصف ساعة noS isaʾa

half board نص بورد noS bord

half past... ونص ...wi noS

half-litre نصف لتر noS litr

half price/fare نصف الثمن Zon
ittaman

hammer شاكوش shakoosh (m)

hand يد yed (m)

» hand luggage شنطة يد shanTit
yed (f)

» hand made مصنوع يدويا maSnooʾa
yedawayan

hand bag شنطة هاندباج shanTa
handibag (f)

handkerchief منديل mandeel (m)

handle اكرة okra (f)

to hang up: he/she hangs up
(telephone) يقفل/تقفل السكة yeʾfil/
teʾfilisseka

to happen: it happens يحصل/تحصل
yeHSal/teHSal

happy سعيد/سعيدة saʾeed/saʾeeda

harbour ميناء meena (f)

hard (difficult) صعب/صعبة Saʾab/
Saʾaba; (not soft) جامد/جامدة
gaemid/gamda

hard drive ذاكرة الكمبيوتر zakirit il
kompyootar (f)

hardware shop محل منتجات منزلية
maHal montagaet manzelaya (m)

hat برنيطة bornaeTa (f)

to hate: he/she hates يكره/تكره yekrah/
tekrah

to have: he/she has عنده/عندها ʾandoo/
ʾandaha

hay قش ʾash (m)

hay fever حساسية Hasasaya (f)

he هو howa

head راس raas (m)

headache صداع Sodaa^a (m)

headlight الانوار الامامية il anwar il amamaya (pl)

headphones سماعات sama^aaet (pl)

to heal: he/she heals يشفى/تشفى yeshfi/teshfi

health صحة SeHa (f)

healthy صحي/صحية SeHi/SeHaya

health food shop محل منتجات صحية maHal montagaet SeHaya (m)

to hear: he/she hears يسمع/تسمع yesma^a/tesma^a

hearing سمع sam^aa (m)

» hearing aid سماعة ودن sama^ait wedn (f)

heart attack ازمة قلبية azma 'albaya (f)

heat حرارة Haraara (f)

heater دفاية dafaya (f)

heating تدفئة tedfe'a (f)

heaven الجنة il ganna (f)

heavy ثقيل/ثقيلة te'eel/te'eela

heel كعب ka^ab (m); (shoe) كعب الحذاء ka^ab il Hizae (m)

height الطول iTTool (m)

helicopter هليكوبتر helikobter (m)

hell جهنم gohannam (f)

hello اهلا ahlan

helmet خوذة khowza (f)

help مساعدة mosa^aada (f) » help! ساعدوني sa^adooni

to help: he/she helps يساعد/تساعد yisa^aid/tisa^aid

her هى haya

herb عشب ^aoshb (m)

herbal tea شاى اعشاب shay a^ashaeb (m)

here هنا hena

here is اهو aho

hers بتاعها bita^aha

high عالى/عالية ^aaeli/^aaelya

high chair كرسى عال korsi ^aaeli (m)

to hijack: he/she hijacks يختطف/تختطف yekhtaTif/tekhtaTif

hill ربوة rabwa (f)

him هو howa

Hindu هندو hindoo

to hire: he/she hires يأجر/تأجر ye'agar/tea'gar

his بتاعه bitae^aoo

history تاريخ tareekh (m)

hobby هواية howaya (f)

to hold: he/she holds يمسك/تمسك yemsik/temsik

hole خرم khorm (m)

holiday اجازة agaeza (f) » on holiday فى اجازة fi agaeza

holidays (school etc.) الاجازة المدرسية il agaeza il madrasaya (f)

holy مقدس/مقدسة moqadas/moqadassa

home منزل manzil (m) » at home فى المنزل fil manzil

to go home: he/she goes home يذهب/تذهب الى المنزل yazhab/tazhab ila il manzil

homemade بيتى bayti

to be homesick: he/she is homesick مشتاق/مشتاقة للعودة moshtae'/moshtae'a lil ^aawda

honest امين/امينة ameen/ameena

honeymoon شهر العسل shahr il ^aasal (m)

to hope: he/she hopes يتمنى/تتمنى yatamanna/tatamanna » I hope so اتمنى ذلك atamanna zaelik

horrible بشع/بشعة bashi^a/bashi^aa

horse حصان HoSaan (m)

horse riding ركوب الخيل rokoob il khayl (m)

hospital مستشفى mostashfa (f)

host(ess) الضيف/الضيفة iDDayf (m)/
iDDayfa (f)

hot حار/حارة Har/Hara
(spicy) حراق/حراقة Harae'/Harae'a

hotel هوتيل hotayl (m)

hour ساعة sa'a (f)

house بيت bayt (m)

housework شغل البيت
shogl il bayt (m)

how كيف kayf

» how far? على بعد اية؟ 'ala bo'd
'addi ay

» how long? ياخذ وقت قد اية؟
yaekhod wa't 'addi ay

» how many? كام؟ kaem

» how much? قد اية؟ 'addi ay

» how much does it cost? ثمنة
اية؟ tamanoo 'addi ay

human (being) انسان/انسانة insaen
(m)/insaena (f)

hungry جعان/جعانة ga'aen/ga'aena

to be hungry: he/she is hungry
جعان/جعانة ga'aen/ga'aena

to hunt: he/she hunts يصطاد/تصطاد
yeSTaad/teSTaad

hurry: to be in a hurry
مستعجل/مستعجلة mista'gil/mista'gila

to hurt: he/she hurts يجرح/تجرح
yegraH/tegraH

husband زوج zowg (m)

hut كوخ kookh (m)

hygienic نظيف/نظيفة naDeef/
naDeefa

I

I انا ana (m or f)

ice ثلج talg (m)

ice cream ايس كريم ais kreem (m)

ice cream parlour محل ايس كريم
maHal ais kreem (m)

ice cube مكعب ثلج mok'ab talg (m)

ice rink حلقة التزحلق على الثلج
Hala'it il tazaHloq 'ala it talg (f)

iced coffee قهوة مثلجة 'ahwa
metalliga (f)

icy مثلج/مثلجة metallig/metalliga

idea فكرة fekra (f)

if اذا iza

ill مريض/مريضة mareeD/mareeDa

illness مرض maraD (m)

to imagine: he/she imagines
يتخيل/تتخيل yetkhaiyal/tetkhaiyal

imagination خيال khayael (m)

important مهم/مهمة mohim/mohima

impossible مستحيل/مستحيلة
mostaHeel/mostaHeela

in فى fi

in a hurry مستعجل/مستعجلة
mista'gil/mista'gila

in front of امام amaem

in order to علشان 'alashaen

included يتضمن/تتضمن
yetaDamman/tetaDamman

independent مستقل/مستقلة mostaqil/
mostaqila

indigestion عسر هضم 'osr haDm (m)

industry صناعة Sina'a (f)

infection تلوث talawos

infectious معدي/معدية mo'adi/
mo'adaya

inflamed ملتهب/ملتهبة moltehib/
moltehiba

inflammation التهاب iltihaeb (m)

influenza انفلونزا infloowenza (m)

informal غير رسمي gheyr rasmi

information معلومات ma'alomaet(pl)

» information desk/office
مكتب الاستعلامات maktab
iste'lamaet (m)

injection حقنة Ho'na (f)

to injure: he/she injures يجرح/تجرح
yegraH/tegraH

» injured مصاب/مصابة moSaab/moSaaba

injury إصابة iSaaba (f)

inn فندق fondo' (m)

innocent برىء/بريئة baree'/baree'a

insect حشرة Hashara (f)

» insect bite لسعة حشرة las°it Hashara (f)

» insect repellent مضاد للحشرات moDaad lil Hasharaat (m)

inside داخل daekhil

instant coffee نسكافية neskafay (m)

instead of بدلا من badal min

instructor معلم/معلمة mo°allim (m)/mo°allima (f)

insulin انسولين insooleen (m)

insult أهانة ihaena (f)

insurance تامين ta'meen (m)

» insurance document بوليصة تامين boleeSit ta'meen (f)

to insure: he/she insures يؤمن/تؤمن yo'amin/to'amin

» insured مؤمن عليه/عليها mo'aman °alaiyh/°alaiyha

intelligent ذكى/ذكية zaki/zakaya

interest (money) ربح rebH (m)

interested مهتم/مهتمة mohtam/mohtama

interesting مثير للإهتمام/مثيرة للإهتمام motheer/motheera lil ihtimaem

international دولى/دولية dawli/dawlaya

internet انترنيت internet (m)

» internet café انترنيت كافية internet kafay (m)

» internet connection وصلة انترنيت waSlit internet (f)

to interpret: he/she interprets يترجم/تترجم yetargim/tetargim

interpreter مترجم/مترجمة motargim (m)/motargima (f)

interval (theatre etc.) استراحة istiraHa (f)

into فى fi

to introduce: he/she introduces يقدم/تقدم ye'adim/te'adim

invitation دعوة da°awa (f)

to invite: he/she invites يدعو/تدعو yed°ow/ted°ow

Ireland ايرلندا airlanda (f)

Irish ايرلندى/ايرلندية airlandi/airlandaya

iron (metal) حديد Hadeed (m)
(for clothes) مكوة makwa (f)

to iron: he/she irons يكوى/تكوى yekwi/tekwi

is فى fi

» is there…? ...فى... fi…

Islam اسلام islaem (m)

Islamic اسلامى/اسلامية islaemi/islamaya

island جزيرة gezira (f)

IT تكنولوجيا المعلومات teknolojya il ma°aloomaet (f)

itch: I've got an itch عايز/عايزة اهرش °ayiz/°ayza ahrosh

J

jacket جاكتة jaketa (f)

jam مربى merabba (f)

jar برطمان barTamaan (m)

jaw فك fak (m)

jazz جاز jaz (m)

jeans جينز jeenz (m)

jellyfish قنديل البحر 'andeel il baHr (m)

jewellery مجوهرات mogawharaat (pl)

jeweller's جواهرجى gawahergi (m)

Jewish يهودى/يهودية yahoodi/yahoodaya

job وظيفة waZeefa (f)

jogging يجرى yegri (m)

joke نكتة *nokta* (f)

journalist صحفي/صحفية *SaHafi* (m)/ *SaHafaya*

journey رحلة *reHla* (f)

judge قاضي *'aaDi* (m)

jug شفشق *shafsha'* (m)

juice عصير *aSeer* (m)

to jump: he/she jumps ينط/تنط *yenoT/ tenoT*

jumper بلوفر *bolowver* (m)

junction ملتقى *moltaqa* (f)

just (only) بس *bas*

K

to keep: he/she keeps يحتفظ/تحتفظ *yeHtafiZ/teHtafiZ*

>> keep to the right الزم اليمين *ilzam il yemeen*

kettle براد *baraad* (m)

key مفتاح *moftaeH* (m)

key ring عليقة مفاتيح *olay'it mafateeH* (f)

kidney كلوة *kelwa* (f)

to kill: he/she kills يقتل/تقتل *ye'til/te'til*

kilo(gram) كيلوجرام *keelogram* (m)

kilometre كيلومتر *keelometr* (m)

kind (sort) نوع *no*; (generous) طيب/ طيبة *Taiyib/Taiyiba*

king ملك *malik* (m)

kiss بوسة *bowsa* (f)

to kiss: he/she kisses يبوس/تبوس *yiboos/tiboos*

kitchen مطبخ *maTbakh* (m)

knee ركبة *rokba* (f)

knickers لباس *libaes* (m)

knife سكينة *sikeena* (f)

knot عقدة *o'da* (f)

to know: he/she knows يعرف/تعرف *ye araf/te raf*

>> I don't know مش عارف/عارفة *mish erif/ arfa*

L

label تيكت *tikit* (m)

lace دانتيل *dantayl* (m)

ladder سلم *sellim* (m)

lady سيدة *saiyeda* (f)

ladies سيدات *saiyidaet* (pl)

lager بيرة *beera* (f)

lake بحيرة *boHayra* (f)

lamb (meat) لحمة ضاني *laHma Daani*

lamp لمبة *lamba* (f)

lamp post عامود نور *amood noor* (m)

land أرض *arD* (f)

to land: he/she lands يهبط/تهبط *yehbaT/tehbaT*

landing (ship etc.) هبوط *hobooT* (m)

landlady صاحبة البيت *SaHbit il bayt* (f)

landlord صاحب البيت *SaHib il bayt* (m)

language لغة *logha* (f)

laptop لابتوب *labtob* (m)

large كبير/كبيرة *kibeer/kibeera*

last اخير/اخيرة *akheer/akheera*

to last: he/she lasts يدوم/تدوم *yedoom/tedoom*

late متأخر/متأخرة *met'akhar/ met'akhara*

later بعدين *ba dayn*

laugh ضحكة *DeHka* (f)

to laugh: he/she laughs يضحك/تضحك *yeDeHak/teDehak*

launderette غسالة *ghasaella* (f)

laundry غسيل *ghaseel* (m)

law القانون *il qanoon* (m)

lawyer محامي/محامية *moHaemi/ moHamaya*

lazy كسلان/كسلانة *kaslaen/kaslaena*

leaf ورقة wara'a (f)

leaflet منشور manshoor (m)

to learn: he/she learns يتعلم/تتعلم
yet°alim/tet°alim

least: at least على الاقل °alal a'al

leather جلد geld (m)

leather goods مصنوعات جلدية
maSnoo°aet geldaya (pl)

to leave: he/she leaves (go away)
يسافر/تسافر yisaefir/tisaefir;
(forget something) ينسى/تنسى
yensa/tensa

lecture محاضرة moHaDra (f)

left شمال shimael

left luggage office مكتب الشنط المخزونة
maktab ishshonaaT il makhzoona (m)

leg رجل regl (m)

legal قانوني/قانونية qanooni/
qanoonaya

leisure وقت الفراغ wa't il faragh (m)

lemon ليمون laemoon (m)

lemonade ليموناتة limonaeta (f)

to lend: he/she lends يسلف/تسلف
yesallif/tesallif

length طول Tool (m)

lens (camera) عدسة °adasa (f)
(contact) عدسة لاصقة
°adasa laSeqa (f)

lentil عدس °ads (m)

less اقل a'al

lesson درس dars (m)

to let: he/she lets (allows) يسمح/تسمح
yesmaH/tesmaH; (rent) يأجر/تأجر
ye'agar/te'agar

letter (to someone) خطاب
khiTaab (m); (of alphabet) حرف
Harf abgadi (m) ابجدى

letterbox صندوق بريد Sandoo'
bareed (m)

level (height, standard) مستوى
mostawa (f)

(flat) مسطح/مسطحة misaTaH/
misaTaHa

level crossing مزلقان mazla'aen (m)

library مكتبة maktaba (f)

licence (driving etc.) رخصة rokhSa (f)

lid غطاء ghaTa (m)

to lie down: he/she lies down
يستلقي/تستلقي yestalqi/testalqi

life حياة Haiyah (f)

lifeboat قارب نجاة 'aerib nagaeH (m)

lifeguard عامل انقاذ °amil inqaaz (m)

lifejacket جاكتة النجاة jakettit
innagaeH (f)

lift اسانسير asansayr (m)

to lift: he/she lifts يرفع/ترفع yerfa°/
terfa°

light (car) كشاف السيارة kashaef
issaiyaara (m)
» light bulb لمبة lamba (f)

light (colour) فاتح/فاتحه faetiH/fatHa
(weight) خفيف/خفيفة khafeef/
khafeefa

to light: he/she lights ينور/تنور
yenawar/tenawar

lighter fuel بنزين الولاعة benzeen il
wala°a (m)

lightning برق barq (m)

to like: he/she likes يحب/تحب yeHeb/
teHeb

limited محدود/محدودة maHdood/
maHdooda

line خط khaT (m)

lion اسد asad (m)

lip شفة sheffa (f)

lipstick قلم روج 'alam rooj (m)

liqueur ليكير likayr (m)

liquid سائل sae'il (m)

list لستة lista (f)

to listen: he/she listens (to)
يسمع/تسمع yesma°/tesma°

litre لتر litr (m)

litter زبالة *zibae*la (f)

little صغير/صغيرة *Soghaiyar/ Soghaiyara*

» a little قليل *'aleel*

to live: he/she lives يعيش/تعيش *ye*ᵃ*eesh/te*ᵃ*eesh*

liver كبدة *kebda* (f)

living-room حجرة الجلوس *Hogrit il goloos* (m)

loan سلفة *solfa* (f)

local محلي/محلية *maHali/maHalaya*

lock ترباس *terbaes* (m)

to lock: he/she locks يترباس/تترباس *yeterbis/teterbis*

locker دولاب صغير *doolaeb Soghaier* (m)

lonely وحيد/وحيدة *waHeed/waHeeda*

long طويل/طويلة *Taweel/Taweela*

(a) long time فترة طويلة *fatra Taweela*

long-distance مسافة طويلة *masaefa Taweela* (f)

» long-distance call مكالمة من مكان بعيد *mokalma min makaen b*ᵃ*eed* (f)

to look: he/she looks (at) ينظر/تنظر *yenZor/tenZor*

he/she looks for يبحث/تبحث عن *yabHas/tabHas* ᵃ*an*

loose سايب/سايبة *saiyib/saiyba*

lorry لوري *loori* (m)

to lose: he/she loses يفقد/تفقد *yefqed/ tefqed*

lost مفقود/مفقودة *mafqood/ mafqooda*

» lost property office مكتب المفقودات *maktab il mafqoodaet* (m)

a lot (of) كثير من *kateer min*

lotion لوسيون *loosyown* (m)

lottery لوتاريا *lotaraya* (f)

loudness صوت عال *Sowt* ᵃ*ali* (m)

lounge صالون *Salown* (m)

to love: he/she loves يحب/تحب *yeHebg/teHeb*

low واطي/واطية *waaTi/waaTya*

low-fat قليل الدهن *'aleel iddehn* (m)

lower اقل *a'al*

lucky: he/she is lucky محظوظ/محظوظة *maHZooZ/maHZooZa*

luggage عفش *ᵃafsh* (pl)

lump كتلة *kotla* (f)

lunch غداء *ghada* (f)

M

machine ماكينة *makkana* (f)

mad مجنون/مجنونة *magnoon/ magnoona*

magazine مجلة *megalla* (f)

mail بوسطة *bosTa* (f)

main اساسي/اساسية *asaesi/asasaya*

» main station المحطة الرئيسية *il maHaTa irra*ᵃ*esaya* (f)

to make: he/she makes يعمل/تعمل *ye*ᵃ*amil/te*ᵃ*amil*

make-up ماكياج *makiyaaj* (m)

male ذكر *zakar*

man رجل *raagil* (m)

manager مدير/مديرة *modeer* (m)/ *modeera* (f)

managing director مدير عام *moodeer* ᵃ*aem*

many كثير *kiteer*

» not many مش كثير *mish kiteer*

map خريطة *khareeTa* (f)

marble رخام *rokhaem* (m)

margarine مارجرين *margareen* (m)

market سوق *soo'* (m)

marmalade مربة لارنج *merabbit lareng* (f)

married متجوزة/متجوز *motazawig/ motazawiga*

» he/she gets married يتجوز/تتجوز *yetzawig/tetazawig*

mascara مسكرة *maskara* (f)

M

mask (diving) قناع qinaᵃ (m)

mass (church) قداس qodaes (m)

match كبريت kabreet (m)
(game) ماتش mutch (m)

material قملش ᵒomaesh (m)

mathematics رياضة riyaaDa (f)

matt (finish) مطفي/مطفية maTfi/
maTfaya

matter: it doesn't matter
مش مهم/مش مهمة mish mohim/
mish mohima

» what's the matter? في اية؟ fi ay

mattress مرتبة martaba (f)

» air mattress مرتبة هواء martabit
hawa (f)

mature ناضج/ناضجة naaDig/naDga

me انا ana

meal وجبة wagba (f)

mean: what does this mean?
اية يعني دة؟ ay yaᵃnni da

meanwhile بينما baynama

measles حصبة HaSba (f)

» German measles حصبة المانية
HaSba almanaya (f)

to measure: he/she measures
يقيس/تقيس yeᵒees/teᵒees

measurement مقاس maᵒaes (m)

meat لحمة laHma (f)

mechanic ميكانيكي mikaneeki (m)

medical طبي Tebbi (m)

medicine (drug) دواء dawa (m)
(subject) طب Teb (m)

medieval من القرون الوسطى min il
qoroon il wosTa

Mediterranean البحر الابيض المتوسط
il baHr il abyaD il motawasiT (m)

medium (size) متوسط/متوسطة
motawasiT/motawaseTa;
(steak) مطبوخة على الريحة
maTbookha ᵃala il reeHa

meeting مقابلة moᵒabla (f)

melon شمامة shamaema (f)

member عضو/عضوة ᵒoDw (m)/
ᵒoDwa (f)

memory ذاكرة zaekira (f)

memory card كارت ذاكرة
kart zaekira (f)

men رجال riggaela (pl)

to mend: he/she mends يصلح/تصلح
yeSallaH/teSallaH

menu منيو menyoo (m)

message رسالة risaella (f)

metal معدن maᵃdan (m)

meter عداد ᵃadaed (m)

metre متر metr (m)

microwave oven فرن ميكروويف forn
mikrowayv (m)

midday في نصف اليوم fi noS il yowm

middle وسط wesT (m)

middle-aged في منتصف العمر fi
montaSaf il ᵃomr

midnight في نصف الليل fi noS il layl

migraine صداع شديد Sodaᵃ
shedeed (m)

mild ضعيف/ضعيفة Daᵃeef/Daᵃeefa

mile ميل meel (m)

milk لبن laban (m)

milkshake ميلك شيك milk shayk (m)

mince لحم مفروم laHma
mafrooma (f)

mind: do you mind if...? عندك مانع؟
ᵃandak/ᵃandik maneᵃ

» I don't mind ما عنديش مانع...
maᵃandeesh maneᵃ

mine (of me) بتاعي/بتاعتي bitaeᵃi
(m)/bitaᵃti (f)

minibar ميني بار minibar (m)

minibus ميني باص minibas (m)

minute (time) دقيقة diᵃeeᵃa (f)

mirror مراية miraya (f)

miscarriage سقوط الحمل soᵒooT il
Haml (m)

202

Miss انسة aenissa (f)

to miss: he/she misses (bus etc.) فتني/فاتتني fatni/fatetni; واحشني/واحشاني (nostalgia) waHeshni/waHshaeni

mist ضباب Dabaab (m)

mistake خطأ khaTa' (m)

to make a mistake يغلط/تغلط yeghlaT/ teghlaT

mixed مخلوط/مخلوطة makhlooT/ makhlooTa

mobile phone موبايل mowbaiyl (m)

model موديل modayl (m)

modem موديم mowdim (m)

modern مودرن modern (m or f)

moisturiser كريم مرطب kraym moraTib (m)

moment لحظة laHZa (f)

monastery دير dayr (m)

money فلوس filoos (pl)

month شهر shahr (m)

monthly شهريا shahrayan

monument نصب تذكاري naSb tizkaeri (m)

moon قمر amar (m)

moped فسبة vespa (f)

more اكثر aktar

» no more كفاية كدة kifaya keda

morning صباح SabaH (m)

mosque جامع gamiª (m)

mosquito ناموسة namoosa (f)

most (of) معظم moªZam

mother ام om (f)

mother-in-law حماة Hama (f)

motor موتور motowr (m)

motorbike موتوسيكل motosekl (m)

motorboat لنش lansh (m)

motor racing سباق سيارات sibae' saiyaraat (m)

motorway اوتوستراد otostraad (m)

mountain جبل gabal (m)

mountaineering تسلق الجبال tasaloª iggibael (m)

mouth فم fam (m)

to move: he/she moves يتحرك/تتحرك yetHarak/tetHarak

» he/she moves house يعزل/تعزل yeªazil/teªazil

MP3-player جهاز ام بى ثرى gihaez embi three

Mr السيد issaiyid

Mrs السيدة issaiyeda

much كثير/كثيرة kiteer/kiteera

» not much مش كثير mish kiteer

mug (cup) فنجال fingael (m)

to mug: he/she mugs (someone) يعتدى/تعتدى yeªatedi/teªatedi

museum متحف matHaf (m)

music موسيقى moseeqa (f)

musical (adj.) موسيقى/موسيقيه moseeqi/moseeqaya

musician موسيقار moseeqar (m)

Muslim مسلم/مسلمة moslim/moslima

must: you must لابد laebod

mystery لغز loghz (m)

N

nail (finger) ظفر Dofr (m)

nail clippers/scissors مقص ma'aS (m)

nail file مقلم اظافر ma'allam aZafir (m)

nail polish مانيكير manikayr (m)

nail polish remover مزيل للمانيكير mozeel lil manikeer (m)

naked عريان/عريانة ªeryaen/ªeryaena

name اسم ism (m)

» my name is... ...اسمى ismi

» what is your name? اسمك اية؟ ismak ay

napkin منديل سفرة mandeel sofra (m)

nappy لفة laffa (f)

» disposable nappy بمبرز bambers

national قومى/قومية *qawmi/ qawmaya*

nationality جنسية *gensaya* (f)

natural(ly) طبيعى/طبيعية *Tabee°ee/ Tabee°aya*

naughty شقى/شقية *shae'i/sha'aya*

nausea قىء *qay'* (m)

navy البحرية *il baHaraya* (f)

navy blue ازرق كحلى *azra' koHli* (m)

near قريب *'areeb*

» nearby قريب/قريبة *'oraiyib/ 'oraiyiba*

nearest أقرب *a'rab*

nearly على وشك *°ala washak*

necessary ضرورى/ضرورية *Daroori/ Darooraya*

neck رقبة *ra'aba* (f)

necklace عقد *°o'd* (m)

to need: he/she needs يحتاج/تحتاج *yeHtaeg/teHtaeg*

needle ابرة *ebra* (f)

negative (photo) النيجاتيف *innegateev* (m)

neighbour جار/جارة *gaar* (m)/ *gaara* (f)

neither ... nor ولا...لا *la ... wala...*

nephew (brother's son) ابن اخويا *ibn akhooya* (m); (sister's son) ابن اختى *ibn okhti*

nervous متوتر/متوترة *motawatir/ motawatira*

net شبكة *shabaka* (f)

never أبداً *abadan*

new جديد/جديدة *gideed/gideeda*

» New Year's Day راس السنة الجديدة *raas issana il gideeda* (f)

news اخبار *akhbaar* (pl)

newspaper جورنال *gornal* (m)

newspaper kiosk كشك الجرائد *koshk il garaiyid* (m)

next اللى جاى/جاية *illi gaiy/gaiya*

» next week الاسبوع اللى جاى *il isboo° illi gaiy*

» next month الشهر اللى جاى *ishshahr illi gaiy*

» next year السنة اللى جاية *issana illi gaiya*

next to بجانب *bigaenib*

nice حلو/حلوة *Helw/Helwa*

niece (brother's daughter) بنت اخويا *bint akhooya* (f); (sister's daughter) بنت اختى *bint okhti* (f)

night ليلة *layla* (f)

nightclub نادى ليلى *naedi layli* (m)

no لا *la*

no longer/no more كفاية *kifaya*

nobody ولا حد *wala Had*

noise ضوضاء *DawDa'* (pl)

noisy دوشة *dawsha*

non-alcoholic غير كحولى *ghayr koHooli*

none ولا حاجة *wala Haga*

non-smoking لغير المدخنين *lighayr il modakhineen*

normal طبيعى/طبيعية *Tabee°ee/ Tabee°aya*

» normally من الطبيعى *min il Tabee°ee*

north شمال *shamael* (m)

nose مناخير *manakheer* (m)

nosebleed نزيف الأنف *nezeef il 'anf* (m)

note (bank) بنك نوت *bank nowt* (m)

nothing ولا شىء *wala shae'*

» nothing else ولا حاجة تانى *wala Haga taeni*

now دلوقتى *dilwa'ti*

nuclear power الطاقة النواوية *iTTaa'a il nawawaya* (f)

number رقم *raqam* (m)

nurse ممرض/ممرضة *momarriD* (m)/ *momarriDa* (f)

nuts مكسرات *mikassaraat* (pl)

O

occasionally احيانا *aHyaenan*

occupied (seat) محجوز/محجوزة *maHgooz/maHgooza*

odd غريب *ghareeb*

of course طبعا *Tab'an*

off (tv, light) مطفى/مطفية *maTfi/maTfaya*; (milk etc.) بايظ/بايظة *baiyZ/baiyZa*

offended اتهان/اتهانت *it-haen/it-haenit*

offer عرض *'arD* (m)
» special offer عرض خاص *'arD khaaS*

office مكتب *maktab* (m)

official رسمى/رسمية *rasmi/rasmaya*

often كثيرا *katheeran*
» how often? قد ايه؟ *'addi ay*

oil زيت *zayt* (m)

OK اوكى *owkay*

old قديم/قديمة *'adeem/'adeema*

old-fashioned دقة قديمة *da'a 'adeema* (f)

olive زيتونة *zaytoona* (f)
» olive oil زيت زيتون *zayt zaytoon* (m)

on على *'ala*

once مرة *marra* (f)

one واحد/واحدة *waHid/waHda*

one-way street طريق اتجاه واحد *Taree' itigaeh waHid* (m)

only فقط *faqaT*

open مفتوح/مفتوحة *maftooH/maftooHa*

to open: he/she opens يفتح/تفتح *yeftaH/teftaH*

operation عملية *'amalaya* (f)

opinion راى *ra'i* (m)
» in my opinion فى راى *fi ra'i*

opposite ضد *Ded*

optician نظاراتى *naDaraati* (m)

or او *aw*

orange (fruit) برتقال *borto'aen* (colour) برتقالى *borto'aeni*

orchestra اوركسترا *orkestra* (f)

to order: he/she orders يطلب/تطلب *yoTlob/toTlob*

ordinary عادى/عادية *'adi/'adaya*

organic food اكل عضوى *akl 'oDwi* (m)

to organise: he/she organises ينظم/تنظم *yenaZam/tenaZam*

original(ly) اصلا *aSlan*
» original language film فيلم باللغة الاصلية *film bilogha il aSlaya* (m)

other اخر *akhar*

others اخرين *akhareen*

ours بتاعنا *bita'ana*

out (of) خارج *khaerig*

out of order لايعمل *la ya'mal*

outdoor/outside خارجى/خارجية *khaerigi/kharigaya*

outdoors خارج البيت *khaerig il bayt*

over فوق *fo'*

owe: how much do I owe (you)? علية لك كام؟ *'alaya leek kaem*

owner مالك *maelik* (m)/مالكة *maelka* (f)

ozone-friendly صديق للاوزون *Sadeeq lil owzown* (m)

ozone layer طبقة الاوزون *Taba'it il owzown* (f)

P

pacemaker عداد دقات القلب *'adaed da'aet il 'alb* (m)

packet باكو *baekoo* (m)

padlock قفل *efl* (m)

page صفحة *SafHa* (f)

painful مؤلم/مؤلمة *mo'lim/mo'lima*

painkiller مزيل للالم *mozeel lil 'alam* (m)

painter (artist) رسام *rasaem* (m)

painting (art) رسم *rasm* (m)

pair زوج *zowg* (m)

palace قصر *'aSr* (m)

pale شاحب/شاحبة *shaeHib/shaeHiba*

pants لباس *libaes* (m)

paper ورق *wara'* (m)

paralysed مشلول/مشلولة *mashlool/ mashloola*

parcel طرد *Tard* (m)

pardon? بعد اذنك *ba*ᵃ*d iznak* (to m)/ *iznik* (to f)

parents اولياء الامور *awliyae' il omoor* (pl)

park جنينة *ginayna* (f)

parking ركن العربية *rakn il* ᵃ*arabaya* (m)

» parking meter عداد الركن ᵃ*adaed il rakn* (m)

parliament برلمان *barlamaen* (m)

particular: in particular بالزات *bilzaet*

partly جزئياً *goz'ayan*

partner شريك/شريكة *shireek* (m)/ *shireeka* (f)

party حفلة *Hafla* (f); (political) حزب *Hezb* (m)

to pass: he/she passes (on road) يمر/تمر *yemor/temor*; (exam, test) ينجح/تنجح *yengaH/tengaH*

passenger راكب/راكبة *raekib/raekiba*

passport جواز سفر *gawaez safar* (m)

» passport control رقابة الجوازات *reqaabit il gawazaet* (f)

past ماضي *maaDi* (m)

» in the past في الماضي *fil maaDi*

pasta مكرونة *makarowna* (f)

pastry فطيرة *fiTeera* (f)

path طريق *Taree'* (m)

patient (adj.) صبور/صبورة *Saboor/ Saboora*; (hospital) مريض/مريضة *mareeD* (m)/*mareeDa* (f)

pattern بطرون *baTrown* (m)

pavement رصيف *raSeef* (m)

to pay: he/she pays يدفع/تدفع *yedfa*ᵃ/ *tedfa*ᵃ

pedal بدال *baddael* (m)

pedestrians مشاة *mooshaeh* (pl)

pedestrian crossing عبور مشاة ᵃ*oboor mooshaeh* (m)

peg مشبك *mashbak* (m)

pen قلم حبر *'alam Hebr* (m)

pencil قلم رصاص *'alam roSaaS* (m)

penfriend مراسل/مراسلة *moraasil* (m) /morasila* (f)

penicillin بنسلين *bansileen* (m)

pension معاش *ma*ᵃ*aesh* (m)

» on a pension على المعاش ᵃ*ala il ma*ᵃ*aesh* (m or f)

people ناس *naes* (pl)

pepper فلفل *filfil* (m)

peppermint نعناع *ne*ᵃ*nae*ᵃ (m)

perfect كامل/كاملة *kaemil/kamla*

performance عرض ᵃ*arD* (m)

perfume برفان *barfaen* (m)

perhaps يمكن *yemkin*

period (menstrual) عادة شهرية ᵃ*aeda shahraya* (f)

» period pains الام العادة *alaem il* ᵃ*aeda* (m)

permit اذن *izn* (m)

person شخص *shakhS* (m or f)

personal شخصي/شخصية *shakh*Si/ *shakhSaya*

petrol بترول *betrowl* (m)

petrol station محطة بنزين *maHaTit benzeen* (f)

phone card كارت تليفون *kart tilifown* (m)

photocopy صورة *Soora* (f)

photo صورة *Soora* (f)

phrase book كتيب عبارات *kotaiyib* ᵃ*ebaraat* (m)

piano بيانو *beeyaeno* (m)

to pick: he/she picks (chooses) يختار/تختار *yekhtaar/tekhtaar*; (flowers etc.) يقطف/تقطف *yo'Tof/ to'Tof*

picnic نزهة nozha (f)

picture صورة Soora (f)

piece قطعة qeTªa (f)

pier رصيف raSeef (m)

pig خنزير/خنزيرة khanzeer (m)/ khanzeera (f)

pill برشاعمة bershaema (f)

» the pill حبوب منع الحمل Hoboob manª il Haml (pl)

pillow مخدة makhadda (f)

pillowcase كيس مخدة kees makhadda (f)

pilot طيار Taiyaar (m)

pin دبوس daboos (m)

pink بمبة bamba (f)

pipe (drain) ماسورة masoora (f) (smoking) بيبة beeba (f)

place مكان makaen (m) (seat) كرسي korsi (m)

plain (adj.) سادة saeda (m or f)

plane طيارة Taiyaara (f)

plant نبات nabaet (pl)

plaster بلاستر blaster (m)

plastic بلاستيك blastik (m)

plastic bag شنطة بلاستيك shanTa blastik (f)

plate طبق Taba' (m)

platform رصيف raSeef (m)

play (theatre) مسرحية masraHaya (f)

to play: he/she plays يلعب/تلعب yelªab/telªab

please من فضلك min faDlak (to m)/ faDlik (to f)

pleased سعيد/سعيدة saªeed/saªeeda (m)

plenty كثير kiteer

pliers كماشة kamaesha (f)

plug (bath) سدادة sadaeda (f) (electrical) فيشة feesha (f)

plumber سباك sabbaek (m)

pneumonia التهاب رئوى iltihaeb re'awi (m)

pocket جيب gayb (m)

poison سم sem (m)

poisonous مسموم/مسمومة masmoom/masmooma

police بوليس bolees (pl)

» police car عربية البوليس ªarabayit il bolees (f)

» police station قسم البوليس 'ism il bolees (m)

polish دهان dahaen (pl)

polite مهذب/مهذبة moªaddab/ moªaddaba

politician سياسي/سياسية seeyaesi (m) /seeyasaya (f)

political سياسي/سياسية seeyaesi (m)/ seeyasaya (f)

politics سياسة seeyaesa (f)

polluted ملوث/ملوثة molawath/ molawatha

pollution تلوث talawath (m)

pool (swimming) حمام سباحة Hamaem sibaHa (f)

poor فقير/فقيرة fa'eer/fa'eera

pop music موسيقى غربية moseeqa gharbaya (f)

Pope البابا il baabaa (m)

popular شعبي/شعبية shaªabi/ shaªabaya

port (harbour) ميناء meena (f)

portable قابل للحمل qaabil lil Haml

porter شيال shaiyael (m)

portion جزء goz' (m)

positive ايجابي/ايجابية igaebi/igabaya

possible ممكن momkin

possibly من الممكن min il momkin

post بوسطة bosTa (f)

to post: he/she posts يرسل/ترسل yersil/tersil

postbox صندوق بريد Sandoo' bareed (m)

postcard كارت بريد kart bareed (m)

P

postcode الرقم البريدي *irraqam il bareedi* (m)

postman ساعى البريد *sa°ee il bareed* (m)

post office مكتب البريد *maktab il bareed* (m)

to postpone: he/she postpones يؤجل/تؤجل *ye°aggil/te°aggil*

pot حلة *Halla* (f)

potato بطاطس *baTaaTis* (pl)

» potato crisps بطاطس شيبسى *baTaaTis shibs* (pl)

pottery خزف *khazaf* (m)

potty (child's) قصرية *°aSraya* (f)

pound (sterling) (استرلينى) جنية *ginay* (*isterleeni*)

to pour: he/she pours يدلق/تدلق *yedlo°/tedlo°*

powder بودرة *bodra* (f)

power (electricity) تيار *taiyaar* (m) (strength) قوة *°owa* (f)

power cut انقطاع فى التيار الكهربائى *inqeTaa° fittaiyaar il kahrobae'i* (m)

pram عربية اطفال *°arabayit aTfaal* (f)

to prefer: he/she prefers يفضل/تفضل *yefaDal/tefaDal*

pregnant حامل *Haemil*

prescription روشتة *roshetta* (f)

present (gift) هدية *hedayya* (f)

press (newspapers) الصحافة *iSSaHaafa* (f)

to press: he/she presses يضغط/تضغط *yeDghaT/teDghaT*

pressure ضغط *DaghT* (m)

pretty حلو/حلوة *Helw/Helwa*

price ثمن *taman* (m)

priest قسيس *°asees* (m)

prime minister رئيس/رئيسة الوزراء *ra'ees* (m)/*ra'eesit* (f) *il wozara'*

prince امير *ameer* (m)

princess اميرة *ameera* (f)

print (photo) طبعة *Tab°a* (f)

to print: he/she prints يطبع/تطبع *yeTba°/teTba°*

prison سجن *segn* (m)

private خاص/خاصة *khaaS/khaaSa*

prize جائزة *gayiz* (f)

probably جايز *gayiz*

problem مشكلة *moshkila* (f)

product منتج *montag* (m)

profession مهنة *mehna* (f)

professor استاذ/استاذة *ostaez* (m)/*ostaeza* (f)

profit ربح *rebH* (m)

programme برنامج *bernaemig* (m)

prohibited ممنوع *mamnoo°*

to promise: he/she promises يوعد/توعد *yow°id/tow°id*

to pronounce: he/she pronounces يستهجى/تستهجى *yestahagga/testahagga*

property ملك *melk* (m)

protestant بروتستنتى/بروتستنتية *brotostanti/brotostantaya*

public (adj.) عام/عامة *°aem/°amma* (noun) الشعب *ishsha°b* (m)

public holiday أجازة قومية *agaeza qawmaya* (f)

to pull: he/she pulls يجذب/تجذب *yegzib/tegzib*

to pump up: he/she pumps up (tyre) ينفخ/تنفخ *yonfokh/tonfokh*

puncture خرم *khorm* (m)

pure نقى/نقية *naqi/naqaya*

purple (adj.) بنفسجى/بنفسجية *benefsegi/benefsegaya*

purse كيس *kees* (m)

to push: he/she pushes يدفع/تدفع *yedfa°/tedfa°*

push-chair عربية اطفال *°arabayit aTfaal* (m)

to put down: he/she puts down ينزل/تنزل *yenezzil/tenezzil*

dictionary

208

to put on: he/she puts on (clothes)
يلبس/تلبس yelbis/telbis
pyjamas بيجاما bijaema (f)

Q

quality قيم/قيمة 'aiyim/'aiyima
quarter ربع rob°a (m)
quay لسان lisaen (m)
queen ملكة malika (f)
question سؤال soo'ael (m)
queue طابور Taboor (m)
quick(ly) يسرعة bisor°a
quiet هادئ/هادئة haedi/hadya
quite جدا gedan

R

rabbi حاخام Hakhaem (m)
rabbit ارنب arnab (m)
rabies مرض الكلب maraD il kalb (m)
racecourse ارض السباق arD
issibae' (f)
racing سباق sibae' (m)
racket مضرب maDrab (m)
radiator رادياتير radyatayr (m)
radio راديو radyo (m)
radioactive اشعاعى/شعاعية ish°a°ee/
ish°a°aya
radio station محطة راديو maHaTit
radyo (f)
railway station محطة سكة حديد
maHaTit sekka Hadeed (f)
rain مطر maTar (m)
» it's raining بتمطر bitmaTar
raincoat بالطو المطر balToo
il maTar (m)
ramp مطلع maTl°a (f)
to rape: he/she rapes يغتصب/تغتصب
yaghtaSib/taghtaSib
rare نادر/نادرة naedir/nadra; (steak)
مطبوخة على الريحة maTbookh °ala
irreeHa

rash طفح جلدى TafH geldi (m)
rate (ratio) بنسبة binisbit (f)
(tariff) التعريفة itta°reefa
raw نى/نية nayy/nayya
razor موس moos (m)
razor blade سن الموس sin il moos (m)
to reach: he/she reaches يصل/تصل
yaSil/taSil
to read: he/she reads يقراء/تقرا ye'ra'/
te'ra'
ready جاهز/جاهزة gaehiz/gaehza
real (authentic) اصلى/اصلية aSli/
aSlaya
really صحيح SaHeeH
reason سبب sabab (m)
receipt ايصال eeSaal (m)
reception استقبال istiqbael (m)
receptionist موظفة استقبال
mowaZafit isti'bael (f)
recipe طريقة الطهى Taree'it iTTahi (f)
to recognise: he/she recognises
يتعرف/تتعرف yat°araf/tat°araf
to recommend: he/she recommends
يوصى/توصى yewaSi/tewaSi
to recover: he/she recovers
يشفى/تشفى yeshfa/teshfa
red احمر/حمراء aHmar/Hamra
» Red Cross الصليب الاحمر iSSaleeb
il aHmar (m)
refrigerator ثلاجة talaega (f)
refugee لاجئ/لاجئه laegi' (m)/
laege'a (f)
refund استرداد istirdaed (m)
region منطقة manTe'a (f)
regional محلى/محلية maHali/
maHalaya
to register: he/she registers يسجل/تسجل
yesagil/tesagil
registration (car) تسجيل tasgeel (m)
religion دين deen (m)
to remain: he/she remains يبقى/تبقى
yeb'a/teb'a

to remember: he/she remembers
يفتكر/تفتكر yeftekir/teftekir

to remove: he/she removes يزيل/تزيل
yezeel/tezeel; (tooth) يخلع/تخلع
yekhla³/tekhla³

rent ايجار iygar (m)

to rent: he/she rents يأجر/تأجر
ye'agar/te'agar

to repair: he/she repairs يصلح/تصلح
yeSalaH/teSalaH

to repeat: he/she repeats يعيد/تعيد
ye³eed/te³eed

report تقرير ta'reer (m)

to rescue: he/she rescues ينقذ/تنقذ
yen'iz/ten'iz

reservation حجز Hagz (m)

to reserve: he/she reserves يحجز/تحجز
yeHgiz/teHgiz

reserved محجوز/محجوزة maHgooz/
maHgooza

to rest: he/she rests يستريح/تستريح
yestereeH/testereeH

restaurant مطعم maT³am (m)

result نتيجة nateega (f)

retired متقاعد/متقاعدة motaqa³id/
motaqa³ida

return عودة ³awda (f)
(ticket) رايح جاي raiyiH gaiy

to return: he/she returns يرجع/ترجع
yerga³/terga³

to reverse: he/she reverses (car)
يرجع للوراء/ترجع للوراء yerga³/terga³ li
wara

rheumatism روماتزم romatizm (m)

rice رز roz (m)

rich غني/غنية ghaeni/ghanaya

to ride: he/she rides (bike, horse)
يركب/تركب yerkab/terkab

right يمين yimeen; (correct) صح SaH

to be right حق على Ha' ³ala
» you're right أنت على حق inta/inti
Ha' ³ala

right-hand side على اليمين ³ala il
yimeen

ring (jewellery) خاتم khaetim (m)

ripe مستوي/مستوية mistewi/mistewaya

risk مخاطرة mokhaTra (f)

river نهر nahr (m)

road طريق Taree' (m)

roadworks اعمال الطرق a³mael
iTToro'

roast في الفرن fil forn

to rob: he/she robs يسرق/تسرق yesra'/
tesra'

robbery سرقة ser'a (f)

rock climbing تسلق الجبال tasalo' il
gibael (m)

roof سطح البيت saTH il bayt (m)

roll (bread) رغيف عيش ragheef
³aysh (m)

room أودة owda (f)

rope حبل Habl (m)

rose روز rowz (m)

rotten فاسد/فاسدة faesid/fazda

rough (sea) هايج/هايجة haeyig/hayga
(surface) خشن/خشنة kheshin/
kheshna

round دائري/دائرية dae'eri/dae'eraya

roundabout دوران dawaraan (m)

row (theatre) صف Saf (m)

rowing boat قارب تجديف 'aerib
ta'deef (m)

royal ملكي/ملكية malaki/malakaya

rubbish زبالة zibaela (f)

rucksack شنطة الظهر shanTit
iDDahr (f)

rude وقح/وقحة waqiH/waqiHa

ruins اطلال aTlael (pl)

to run: he/she runs يجري/تجري yegri/
tegri

rush hour ساعة الزروة sae³it
izzarwa (f)

rusty مصدي/مصدية miSaddi/
miSaddaya

S

sad حزين/حزينة Hazeen/Hazeena زعلان/زعلانة z²alaen/z²alaena

safe (strongbox) خزنة khazna (f)

safety pin دبوس مشبك daboos mashbak (m)

sail شراع shira² (m)

sailing ابحار ibHaar (m)

sailing boat فلوكة felooka (f)

sailor بحار baHaar (m)

saint قديس qedees (m)

sale (bargains) اوكازيون okazyown (m)

salt ملح malH (m)

salty مالح/مالحة maeliH/malHa

same زيه zaiyo

sample عينة ²iyenna (f)

sand رمل raml (m)

sandals صندل Sandal (m)

sandwich ساندوتش sandawitch (m)

sanitary towel فوطة صحية fooTa SaHaya (f)

satisfied راضي/راضية raaDi/raaDya

sauce صوص SowS (m)

saucepan حلة Halla (f)

saucer طبق شاي Taba² shay (m)

sauna سونا sowna (f)

to save: he/she saves (money) يوفر/توفر yewafar/tewafar

to say: he/she says يقول/تقول ye²ool/te²ool

scales ميزان mizaen (m)

scarf ايشارب esharb (m)

scenery المنظر il manZar (m)

school مدرسة madrassa (f)

science علوم ²oloom (pl)

scientist عالم/عالمة ²alim (m)/²alma (f)

scissors مقص ma²aS (m)

scooter فسبا vesba (f)

score: what's the score? اية النتيجة ay innateega

Scotland اسكوتلاندا iskotlanda (f)

Scottish اسكوتلاندي/اسكوتلاندية iskotlandi/iskotlandaya

to scratch: he/she scratches يهرش/تهرش yohrosh/tohrosh

screen شاشة shaesha (f)

screw مسمار قلاووز mosmaar ²alawowz (m)

screwdriver مفك mifak (m)

scuba diving الغوص تحت الماء il ghoS taHt il mae²

sculpture نحت naHt (m)

sea بحر baHr (m)

seafood ماكولات بحرية ma²koolaet baHaraya (pl)

seasickness دوار البحر dawaar il baHr (m)

season موسم moosim (m)

season ticket تذكرة موسمية tazkara mawsimaya (f)

seat كرسي korsi (m)

seatbelt حزام المقعد Hizaem il maq²ad (m)

second (time) ثانية sanya (f)

secret سر ser (m)

secretary سكرتيرة sekertayra (f)

section جزء goz² (m)

to see: he/she sees بيشوف/بتشوف yeshoof/teshoof

self-catering (apartment) شقة مجهزة للخدمة الذاتية (sha²a) mogaHaza lil khedma izzataya (f)

self-service الخدمة الذاتية khedma zataya (f)

to sell: he/she sells يبيع/تبيع yebee²/tebee²

to send: he/she sends يبعث/تبعث yeb²at/teb²at

senior citizen مواطن مسن mowaaTen mosen (m)

sensible عاقل/عاقلة ²ae²il/²a²la

sentence (writing) جملة gomla (f)

separate(d) منفصل/منفصلة monfaSil/monfaSila

serious (grave) جاد/جادة gaed/gada (important) مهم/مهمة mohim/mohima

to serve: he/she serve يخدم/تخدم yekhdim/tekhdim

service (charge) ضريبة خدمة Dareebit khedma (f); (church) قداس 'odaes (m)

set price سعر محدد se'r moHadad

several عدة 'eda

to sew: he/she sews يخيط/تخيط yekhaiyaT/tekhaiyaT

sewing خياطة khiyaaTa (f)

sex (gender) جنس gens (m) (intercourse) العلاقة الجنسية il 'elaqa il gensaya (f)

shade: in the shade في الظل fi iDDel

shadow خيال khaeyael (m)

shampoo شامبو shampoo (m)

sharp حامي/حامية Haemi/Hamya

shave حلاقة الذقن Hilae'it idda'n (m)

to shave: he/she shaves يحلق/تحلق yeHla'/teHla'

shaving cream/foam كريم حلاقة kraym Hilae'a (m)

she هي haya

sheep خاروف kharoof (m)

sheet (for bed) ملاية milaya (f) (paper) ورقة wara'a (f)

sheikh (religious leader) شيخ shaykh (m)

shelf رف raf (m)

shell هيكل haykal (m)

shellfish صدفة بحرية Sadafa baHaraya (f)

shelter ملجأ malga' (m)

shiny لامع/لامعة laeme'a (m)/lam'a (f)

ship مركب markib (f)

shirt قميص 'ameeS (m)

shock (electrical) صدمة كهربائية Sadma kahrobae'aya (f) (emotional) صدمة عاطفية Sadma 'aaTifaya (f)

shocked مصدوم/مصدومة maSdoom/maSdooma

shoe(s) جزمة gazma (f)

shoe polish ورنيش احزية warneesh aHzaya (m)

shoe repairer's مصلح الاحذية moSaliH il aHzaya (m)

shoe shop محل الاحزية maHal aHzaya (m)

shoe size مقاس الاحزية ma'aes il aHzaya (m)

shop محل maHal (m)

shop assistant بياع/بياعة baiya' (f)/baiya'a (m)

shopping centre مول mowl (m)

short قصير/قصيرة oSaiyar/oSaiyara

shorts شورت short (m)

shoulder كتف ketf (m)

to shout: he/she shouts يزعق/تزعق yiza'a'/tiza'a'

show عرض 'arD (m)

to show: he/she shows يعرض/تعرض ye'ariD/te'ariD

shower دش dosh (m)

shut مقفول/مقفولة ma'fool/ma'foola

to shut: he/she shuts يغلق/تغلق yeghla'/teghla'

shutter شيش sheesh (m)

sick (unwell) مريض/مريضة mareeD/mareeDa

» he/she is being sick (vomiting) يستفرغ/تستفرغ yestafragh/testafragh

» I feel sick عايز/عايزة استفرغ 'ayiz/'ayza astafragh

sick bag كيس استفراغ kees istifraegh (m)

side جانب gaenib (m)

sight (vision) رؤية ro'iya (f)
(tourist) اماكن سياحية amaekin siyaHaya (f)

sightseeing زيارة الاماكن السياحية ziyaarit il amaekin issiyaHaya (f)

sign علامة ªalaema (f)

to sign: he/she signs يوقع/توقع yewa'ªa/tewa'ªa

signal اشارة ishaara (f)

signature امضاء imDa (f)

sikh سيخ seekh (m)

silence صمت Samt (m)

silk حرير Hareer (m)

silver فضة faDDa (f)

SIM card كارت سيم kart sim (m)

similar مشابه/مشابهة moshaebih/moshabha

simple بسيط/بسيطة baseeT/baseeTa

since منذ monz

to sing: he/she sings يغنى/تغنى yeghanni/teghanni

single (room) غرفة مفردة ghorfa mofrada (f) ; (ticket) تذكرة رايح tazkara raiyH (f) (unmarried) عازب/عازبة ªaezib/ªaezba

sink حوض HowD (m)

sinus infection التهاب الجيوب الأنفية iltihaeb il giyoob il anfayya (m)

sister اخت okht (f)

sister-in-law مرات اخويا miraat akhooya (f)

to sit: he/she sits (down) يقعد/تقعد yo'ªod/to'ªod

size (clothes, shoes) مقاس ma'aes (m)

skates (ice) احزية التزحلق على الثلج aHzayit ittazaHloq ªala il talg (pl)

skimmed milk لبن بدون دهن laban bidoon dehn

skin جلد geld (m)

skirt جونلة gonella (f)

sky سماء sama (f)

to sleep: he/she sleeps ينام/تنام yinaem/tinaem

sleeper/sleeping-car عربة النوم ªarabayit innowm (f)

sleeping bag شنطة النوم shanTit innowm (f)

sleeve كم kom (m)

slices ترنشات transhaat (pl)

slim رفيع/رفيعة rofaiyªa/rofaiyªaa

slippery مزحلق/مزحلقة mizaHla'/mizaHla'a

slow(ly) بشويش bishwaysh

slow down هدى السرعة haddi is sorªa

small صغير/صغيرة Soghaiyar/Soghaiyara

smell رائحة reeHa (f)

to smell: he/she smells يشم/تشم yeshem/teshem (of) رائحة ال.. reeHit il..; (bad/good) رائحتها/رائحته reHtoo/reHetha

to smile: he/she smiles يبتسم/تبتسم yebtessim/tebtessim

smoke دخان dokhaen (m)

to smoke: he/she smokes يدخن/تدخن yedakhan/tedakhan

smooth ناعم/ناعمة naeªim/naªma

to sneeze: he/she sneezes يعطس/تعطس yeªaTas/teªaTas

snorkel امبوبة تنفس amboobit il tanafos (f)

soap صابون Saboon (m)

sock شراب shoraab (m)

socket كوبس kobs (m)

soda (water) صودا Sowda (f)

soft ناعم/ناعمة naeªim/naªma

soft drink مشروب خفيف mashroob khafeef (m)

software سوفتواير softwaer (m)

soldier عسكرى ªaskari (m)

solicitor محامى/محامية moHaemi (m)/moHamaya (f)

solid صلب/صلبة Salb/Salba

S

some بعض baªD

somehow بطريقة او باخري biTaree'a aw bi'okhra

someone ما شخص shakhSin ma

something شيء shae'

sometimes احيانا aHiyaenan

somewhere فى مكان ما fi makaenin ma

son ابن ibn (m)

son-in-law جوز بنتى gowz binti (m)

soon قريب oraiyaib

as soon as possible فى اقرب ما يمكن fi aqrab ma yomkin

sore ملتهب/ملتهبة moltahib/ moltahiba

sorry: I'm sorry اسفة/اسف انا ana aesif (m)/asfa (f)

sound صوت Sowt (m)

soup شربة shorba (f)

sour حامض/حامضة HaamiD/HamDa

south جنوب ganoob

souvenir سوفونير soovoneer (m)

space مكان makaen

spare time وقت فراغ wa't faragh (m)

spare tyre عجلة استبن ªagala istibn (f)

spark plug فيش الصمامات fayesh iSSamaamaat (m)

sparkling wine نبيت فوار nebeet fawaar (m)

to speak: he/she speaks يتكلم/تتكلم yetkalim/tetkalim

special خاص/خاصة khaaS/khaaSa
» special offer عرض خاص ªarD khaaS (m)

speciality تخصص takhaSoS (m)

speed سرعة sorªa (f)

speed limit حدود السرعة Hodood issorªa (pl)

to spend: he/she spends (money) يصرف/تصرف yeSrif/teSrif ; (time) يقضى/تقضى وقت ye'aDi/te'aDi wa't

spice توابل tawaebil (pl)

spicy متبل/متبلة metabbil/metabilla

spinach سبانخ sabaenikh (f)

spirits مشروبات روحية mashroobaat rawHaya (pl)

to spoil: he/she spoils (a child) يدلع/تدلع yedallªa/tedallªa

sponge سفنجة safenga (f)

spoon معلقة maªlaªa (f)

sport رياضة riyaaDa (f)

sprained ملوى/ملوية malwi/malwaya

spray رش rash (m)

spring (season) ربيع rabeeª (m)

square (in town) ميدان midaen (m) (shape) مربع morabbaª (m)

stadium استاد istaed (m)

stain بقعة boªªa (f)

stairs سلم sellim (pl)

stalls (theatre) لوج lowj (m)

stamp (postage) طابع Taabiª (m)

to stand: he/she stands يقف/تقف yo'af/to'af

start بداية bidayya (f)

start: he/she starts يبدا/تبدا yebda'/tebda'

starter(s) (food) مشهيات moshahiyaet (pl)

station محطة maHaTa (f)

stationer's محل ادوات مكتبية maHal adawaet maktabaya (m)

statue تمثال temsael (m)

to stay: he/she stays (remains) يستنى/تستنى yestanna/testanna

steak بفتيك boftaek (m)

to steal: he/she steals يسرق/تسرق yesra'/tesra'

steamed مبخر/مبخرة mobakhar/ mobakhara

steel صلب Solb (m)

steep منحدر/منحدرة monHadir/ monHadira

214

step (footstep) خطوة **khaTwa** (f)
(stairs) سلمة **sellema** (f)

stepbrother اخ غير شقيق **akh ghayr sha'ee'** (m)

stepchildren اخوة غير اشقاء **ekhwat ghayr ashe'aa'** (pl)

stepfather زوج الام **zowg il 'om** (m)

stepmother زوجة الاب **zowgit il ab** (f)

stepsister اخت غير شقيقة **okht ghayr sha'ee'a**

steering wheel دريكسيون **direksyown** (m)

stereo ستريو **steryo** (m)

sterling: pound sterling جنية استريلينى **ginay isterleenee** (f)

steward(ess) مضيف/مضيفة **moDeef** (m)/**modDeefa** (f)

stuck (glued) لازق/لازقة **laezi'/laz'a** (can't be moved) مزنوق/مزنوقة **maznoo'/maznoo'a**

sticky لزاق/لزاقة **lazae'/lazae'a**

stiff صلب/صلبة **Salb/Salba**

still (yet) مازال **mazael**

still (non-fizzy) من غير فوار **min ghayr fawaar**

sting لدغة **ladgha** (f)

to sting: he/she stings يلدغ/تلدغ **yeldogh/teldogh**

stock cube مربع شربة **morabba' shorba** (m)

stock exchange البورصة **il borSa** (f)

stolen مسروق/مسروقة **masroo'/masroo'a**

stomach معدة **me'da** (f)
» stomach ache مغص **maghaS** (m)
» stomach upset نزلة معوية **nazla ma'awaya** (f)

stone طوبة **Tooba** (f)

stop (bus) محطة **maHaTa** (f)

to stop: he/she stops يقف/تقف **yo'af/to'af**

stop! قف! **qef**

stopcock محبس **maHbas** (m)

story رواية **rowaeya** (f)

storey الدور **iddowr** (m)

stove فرن **forn** (m)

straight مستطيلة/مستطيل **mostaTeel/mostaTeela**

straight on على طول **'ala Tool**

strange غريب/غريبة **ghareeb/ghareeba**

strap طوق **Tow'** (m)

straw (drinking) شفاطة **shafaaTa** (f)

strawberries فراولة **farawla** (f)

street شارع **share'** (m)

stretcher نقالة **na'aela** (f)

strike ضربة **Daarba** (f)
» on strike اضراب **iDraab**

string دوبارة **dobaara** (f)

striped مقلم/مقلمة **me'allim/me'allima**

strong قوى/قوية **'awi/'awaiya**

student طالب/طالبة **Taalib** (m)/**Taaliba**

to study: he/she studies يدرس/تدرس **yedris/tedris**

stung اتلدغ/اتلدغت **etladagh/etladaghit**

stupid عبيط/عبيطة **'abeeT/'abeeTa**

style اسلوب **isloob** (m)

subtitled مترجم/مترجمة **motargam/motargama**

suburb ضاحية **DaHaya** (f)

to succeed: he/she succeeds ينجح/تنجح **yengaH/tengaH**

success نجاح **nagaeH** (m)

suddenly فجأة **fag'a**

sugar سكر **sokkar** (m)

sugar lump سكر مكعبات **sokkar mokk'abaet** (m)

suit (clothing) بدلة **badla** (f)

suitcase شنطة **shanTa** (f)

summer الصيف **iSSayf** (m)

sun الشمس *ishshams* (m)

to sunbathe: he/she sunbathes
ياخذ/تاخذ حمام شمس *yaekhod/taekhod Hamaem shams*

sunburn حروق الشمس *Horoo' ishshams* (pl)

sunglasses نظارة شمسية *naDaara shamsaya* (f)

sunny مشمس *moshmis*

sunstroke ضربة شمس *Darbit shams* (f)

suntan اسمرار *ismiraar* (m)

» suntan lotion لوسيون الاسمرار *loosyown il ismiraar* (m)

supermarket سوبرماركت *soobarmarkit* (m)

supper عشاء *ºasha* (m)

supplement اجرة إضافية *ogra iDafaya* (f)

suppose: I suppose so افترض ان *aftariD ºan*

suppository لبوس *lowboos* (m)

sure اكيد *akeed*

surface سطح *saTH* (m)

to surf: he/she surfs the net
يزور/تزور الانترنت *yezoor/tezoor il internet*

surname اسم العائلة *ism il ºayla* (m)

surprise مفاجأة *mowfag'a* (f)

surprised فوجئت *fowge't* (m & f)

surrounded by بى محاط *moHaaT bi*

to swallow: he/she swallows يبلع/تبلع *yeblaºa/teblaºa*

to sweat: he/she sweats يعرق/تعرق *yeºra'/teºra'*

sweeter اطعم *aTºam*

sweet طعم/طعمة *Teºim/Teºma*

sweetener مسكر *mosakkir* (m)

sweets مليس *milabbis* (pl)

swelling ورم *waram* (m)

to swim: he/she swims يعوم/تعوم *yeºoom/teºoom*

swimming pool حمام سباحة *Hamaem sibaHa* (f)

swimming trunks مايو *maiyo* (m)

swimsuit مايو *maiyo* (m)

switch مفتاح *moftaH* (m)

to switch off: he/she switches off يقفل/تقفل *ye'fil/te'fil*

to switch on: he/she switches on يولع/تولع *yewalaºa/tewalaºa*

swollen وارم/وارمة *waerim/warma*

symptoms اعراض المرض *aºraaD il maraD* (pl)

synagogue معبد يهودى *maºbad yahoodi*

synthetic مركب *morakab*

system سيستم *sistim* (m)

T

table طرابيزة *Tarabayza* (f)

table tennis بنج بونج *ping pong* (m)

tablecloth مفرش *mafrash* (m)

tablet حباية *Habaya* (f)

tailor ترزى/خياطة *tarzi* (m)/ *khaiyaTa* (f)

to take: he/she takes يأخذ/تأخذ *yaekhod/taekhod*

» he takes an exam ياخد امتحان *yaekhod imtiHaen*

» he takes a photo ياجد صورة *yaekhod Soora*

» it takes... (time) ياخد...*yaekhod*

to take off: he/she takes off (clothes) يقلع/تقلع *ye'lºa/te'lºa*

take off (plane) اقلاع *iqlºa* (m)

taken (seat etc.) محجوز/محجوزة *maHgooz/maHgooza*

to talk: he/she talks يتكلم/تتكلم *yatkallam/tatkallam*

tall طويل/طويلة *Taweel/Taweela*

tampon صمامة قطنية *Samama 'oTnaya* (f)

tap حنفية *Hanafaya* (f)

tap water مياة من الحنفية *maiya min il Hanafaya* (f)

tape (adhesive) لزاق *lazae'* (m) (cassette) شريط كاسيت *shireeT kasset* (m)

tape measure متر *metr* (m)

tariff تعريفة *ta°reefa* (f)

taste طعم *Ta°m* (m)

to taste: he/she tastes يذوق/تذوق *yedoo'/tedoo'*

tax ضريبة *Dareeba* (f)

taxi تاكسى *taksi* (m)
  » taxi rank موقف تاكسى *maw'af taksi* (m)

tea شاى *shay* (m)

teabag كيس شاى *kees shay* (m)

to teach: he/she teaches يدرس/تدرس *yedris/tedris*

teacher مدرس/مدرسة *moddarris* (m)/ *moddarissa* (f)

team فريق *faree'* (m)

teapot براد *baraad* (m)

tear (rip) يمزق/تمزق *yemaza'/ temaza'* (cry) دمعة *dem°a* (f)

in tears بيبكى/بتبكى *biyebki/bitebki*

teaspoon معلقة شاى *ma°la'it shay* (f)

teat (for baby's bottle) بزازة *bazaeza* (f)

technical فنى/فنية *fanni/fannaya*

technology تكنولوجيا *teknolojya* (f)

teenager مراهق/مراهقة *moraahiq* (m)/*morahqa* (f)

telephone تليفون *tilifown* (m)
  » telephone box كشك تليفون *koshk tilifown* (m)
  » telephone card كارت تليفون *kart tilifown* (m)

  » telephone directory دليل تليفون *daleel tilifown* (m)

to telephone: he/she telephones يتكلم/تتكلم بالتليفون *yetkalim/ tetkalim bil tilifown*

television تلفزيون *televisyown* (m)

to tell: he/she tells يقول/تقول *ye°ool/ te°ool*

temperature حرارة *Haraara* (f)
  » he/she has a temperature عنده/عندها حرارة *°ando/°andaha Haraara*

temporary مؤقت/مؤقتة *mow'aqat/ mow'aqata*

tennis تنس *tenis* (m)

tennis court ملعب تنس *mal°ab tenis* (m)

tent خيمة *khayma* (f)
  » tent peg مشبك خيمة *mashbak khayma* (m)
  » tent pole عامود الخيمة *°amood il khayma* (m)

terminal محطة *maHaTa* (f)

terminus موقف *maw'af* (m)

terrace تراس *terras* (m)

terrible رهيب/رهيبة *raheeb/raheeba*

terrorist ارهابى *irhaebi* (m)/ *irhabaya* (f)

text message رسالة بالتكست *risaella bil tekst* (f)

than من *min*

thank you (very much) شكرا (جزيلاً) *shokran (gazeelan)*

that (one) ده/دى *da/di*

the ال *il*

theatre مسرح *masraH* (m)

theft السرقة *isser'a* (f)

theirs بتاعهم *bita°hom*

them هم *homa*

then وبعدين *wi ba°dayn*

there (is/are) هناك *hinaek*

there it is اهو *aho*

therefore و لذلك *wa lizaelik*

these هؤلاء *ha'oolae'*

they هم *homa*

thick سميك/سميكة *sameek/sameeka*

thief حرامي/ حرامية *Haraami* (m)/ *Haramaya* (f)

thigh فخذ *fakhd* (m)

thin رفيع/رفيعة *rofaiya'a/rofaiya'a*

thing شيء *shae'*

to think: he/she thinks يفكر/تفكر *yefekar/tefekar*

» I (don't) think so (لا) اعتقد *(la) a'taqid*

third ثالثا *thaelithan*

thirsty عطشان/عطشانة *'aTshaan/'aTshaana*

this (one) هذا/هذة *haeza/haezihi*

those هؤلاء *hae'oolae'*

thread خيط *khayT* (m)

threat تهديد *tahdeed* (m)

throat زور *zowr* (m)

through خلال *khilael*

to throw: he/she throws يقذف/تقذف *yaqzif/taqzif*

he/she throws away يرمى/ترمى *yermi/termi*

thumb ابهام *ibhaem* (m)

thunder رعد *ra'ad* (m)

ticket تذكرة *tazkara* (f)

ticket office مكتب حجز التذاكر *maktab Hagz il tazaeker* (m)

tide المد *il mad* (m)

tie كرافتة *karavatta* (f)

tight ضيق/ضيقة *Daiya'/Daiya'a*

tights شراب حريمى *shoraab Hareemi* (pl)

till (until) حتى *Hatta*

time (once etc.) مرة *marra* (f) (general) وقت *wa't* (m)

timetable جدول *gadwal* (m)

tin علبة *'elba* (f)

tin foil ورق الومنيوم *wara' alamonyom* (m)

tinned (food) (اكل) محفوظ *(akl) maHfooZ* (m)

tin opener فتاحة علب *fatahHit 'elab* (f)

tip (in restaurant etc.) بقشيش *ba'sheesh* (m)

tired تعبان/تعبانة *ta'baen/ta'baena*

tissues ورق كلينكس *wara' kleeneks* (m)

to الى *ila*

toast توست *towst* (m)

tobacco طنباق *Tonbaq* (m)

tobacconist بياع السجاير *baiya' issagayer*

today النهاردة *innaharda*

toiletries ادوات الزينة *adawaet izzeena* (pl)

toilet تواليت *twalit* (m)

» toilet paper ورق تواليت *wara' twalit* (m)

toll ضريبة طرق *Dareebit Toro'* (f)

tomato طماطم *TamaaTim* (m)

tomorrow بكرة *bokra*

tongue لسان *lissaen* (m)

tonight الليلة *ilayla* (f)

too كمان *kamaen* (as well) ايضا *aiDan*

tools عدة *'edah* (f)

toolkit عدة الشغل *'edit ishshoghl* (f)

tooth سنة *senna* (f)

toothache وجع سنان *wag'a sinnaen* (m)

toothbrush فرشة سنان *forshit sinnaen* (f)

toothpaste معجون سنان *m'agoon sinnaen* (m)

toothpick مسواك *miswaek* (m)

top (mountain) قمة *qema* (f)

» on top of فوق *fo'*

torch بطارية baTarayya (f)

torn ممزق/ممزقة momazaq/
momazaqa

total اجمالي igmaeli

totally كلية kolayatan

to touch: he/she touches يلمس/تلمس
yelmis/telmis

tough (difficult) صعب/صعبة Saᵃb/
Saᵃba

tour دورة dawra (f)

tourism سياحة siyaHa (f)

tourist سائح/سائحة saeyiH (m)/
sayHa (f)

tourist office مكتب سياحة maktab
siyaHa (m)

tournament دورة رياضية dawra
riyaDaya (f)

towards فى اتجاة fi itigaeh

towel فوطة fooTa (f)

tower برج borg (m)

town مدينة madeena (f)

» town centre وسط البلد wesT il
balad

» town hall البلدية il baladaya (f)

toy لعبة leᵃba (f)

track (race) تراك trak (m)

traditional تقليدى/تقليدية taᵃleedi/
taᵃleedaya

traffic المرور il moroor (m)

traffic jam تكدس المرور takados il
moroor (m)

traffic lights اشارات المرور isharaat il
moroor (pl)

train قطر 'aTr (m)

» by train بالقطر bil 'aTr

trainers ترينر trayner (m)

tram ترام tram (m)

tranquilliser مهدىء mohaddi' (m)

to translate: he/she translates
يترجم/تترجم yetargim/tetargim

translation ترجمة targama (f)

to travel: he/she travels يسافر/تسافر
yesaefir/tesaefir

travel agency وكالة سفر wikaelit
safar (m)

traveller's cheque شيكات سياحية
shikaet siyaHaya (pl)

travel sickness دوار السفر dawaar
issafar (m)

treatment علاج elaeg (m)

tree شجرة shagara (f)

trip رحلة reHla (f)

trousers بنطلون banTalown (m)

true صحيح/صحيحة SaHeeH/SaHeeHa

» that's true هذا صحيح haeza
SaHeeH

to try: he/she tries يحاول/تحاول
yeHawil/teHawil

to try on: he/she tries on يقيس/تقيس
ye'ees/te'ees

t-shirt تيشيرت teeshirt (m)

tube (pipe) انبوبة anbooba (f)
(underground) مترو الانفاق metro il
'anfae' (m)

tuna تونة toona (f)

tunnel نفق nafa' (m)

turn: it's my turn الدور علية iddowr
ᵃalaya

to turn: he/she turns يلف/تلف
yelif/telif

to turn off: he/she turns off يقفل/تقفل
ye'fil/te'fil

turning لفة laffa (f)

twice مرتين marritayn

twin beds سريرين sereerayn

twisted ملتوى/ملتوية moltawi/
moltawaya

type (sort) نوع noᵃ (m)

to type: he/she types يطبع/تطبع
yeTbaᵃ/teTbaᵃ

typical نموذجى/نموذجية namoozagi/
namoozagaya

tyre كاوتش kawetch (m)

U

V

U

USB lead كبل يو اس بي *kabl yoo ess bee* (m)

ulcer قرحة *qorHa* (f)

umbrella شمسية *shamsaya* (f)

uncle (father's brother) عم *ªam* (m)
(mother's brother) خال *khael* (m)

uncomfortable مش مريح/مريحة *mish moreeH/moreeHa*

under تحت *taHt*

underground تحت الارض *taHt il arD*

underpants لباس *libaes* (m)

underpass ممر *mamar* (m)

to understand: he/she understands يفهم/تفهم *yefham/tefham*

underwater تحت الماء *taHt il maiya*

underwear ملابس داخلية *malaebis daekhilaya* (pl)

to undress: he/she undresses يقلع/تقلع *yeªlªa/teªlªa*

unemployed عاطل/عاطلة *ªaTil/ªaTla*

unemployment بطاله *baTaala* (f)

unfortunately لسوء الحظ *lisooª il HaZ* (m)

unhappy مش سعيد/سعيدة *mish saªeed/saªeeda*

uniform الملابس الرسمية *il malabis irrasmaya*

united متحد/متحدة *motaHid/ motaHida*

university جامعة *gaemeªa* (f)

unleaded petrol بنزين بدون رصاص *benzeen bidoon roSaaS* (m)

unlimited غير محدود/محدودة *ghayr maHdood/maHdooda*

unpleasant مش ولابد *mish walabod*

to unscrew: he/she unscrews يفتح/تفتح *yeftaH/teftaH*

until حتى *Hata*

unusual غير عادي *ghayr ªaedi*

unwell تعبان/تعبانة *taªbaen/taªbaena*

up فوق *fo'*

» up the road في اول الشارع *fi awil ishshareª*

upper اعلى *ªala*

upstairs الدور اللي فوق *iddowr illi fo'*

urgent مستعجل/مستعجلة *mistaªgil/ mistaªgila*

urine بول *bowl* (m)

us احنا *eHna*

to use: he/she uses يستخدم/تستخدم *yestekhdim/testekhdim*

useful مفيد/مفيدة *mofeed/mofeeda*

useless مش مفيد/مفيدة *mish mofeed/mofeeda*

usually عادة *ªadatan*

V

vacant فاضي/فاضية *faaDi/faDya*

vacuum cleaner هوفر *hoover* (m)

valid صالح/صالحة *SaaliH/SaaliHa*

valuable قيمة/قيمة *'aiyim/'aiyima*

valuables اشياء قيمة *ashyaª 'aiyima* (pl)

van عربية نص نقل *ªarabaya noS naª'l* (f)

vanilla فانيلا *vanilya* (f)

vase فاسا *vasa* (f)

VAT ضريبة مبيعات *Dareebit mabeeªaet* (f)

vegetarian نباتي/نباتية *nebaeti/ nabataya*

vehicle عربية *ªarabaya* (f)

veil حجاب *Higaeb* (m)

ventilation تهوية *tahwaya* (f)

vertigo الخوف من الاماكن المرتفعة *il khowf min il amaekin il mortafiªa* (m)

very جدا *gedan*

video فيديو *vidyo* (m)

view منظر *manZar* (m)

village قرية *qarya* (f)

vinegar خل khal (m)

vineyard مزارع الكروم mazaeri' il koroom (pl)

virgin عذراء 'azra' (f)

visa فيزا veeza (f)

to visit: he/she visits يزور/تزور yezoor/tezoor

visitor زائر/زائرة zae'ir (m)/zae'ira (f)

vitamin فيتامين vitameen (m)

voice صوت Sowt (m)

volleyball فولي volli (m)

voltage فولت الكهرباء volt il kahrabba

to vomit: he/she vomits يستفرغ/تستفرغ yestafragh/testafragh

W

wafer بسكويت baskaweet (m)

wage الأجرة ogra (f)

waist وسط wesT (m)

to wait: he/she waits (for) ينتظر/تنتظر yantaZir/tantaZir

waiter جارسون garsown (m)

waiting room حجرة الانتظار Hogrit il intiZaar

waitress جارسونة garsowna (f)

Wales ويلز waylz

to (go for a) walk: he/she walks يتمشى/تتمشى yetmasha/tetmasha

wall حيطة HayTa (f)

wallet محفظة maHfaZa (f)

to want: he/she wants عايز/عايزة 'ayiz/'ayza

war حرب Harb (m)

warm دافئ/دافية daefi/dafya

to wash: he/she washes يغسل/تغسل yeghsil/teghsil

washable قابل للغسيل 'aabil lil ghaseel

washbasin حوض HowD (m)

washing غسيل ghaseel

washing machine غسالة ghasaela (f)

washing powder مسحوق صابون الغسيل masHoo' Saboon il ghaseel

washing-up غسيل الصحون ghaseel iSSoHoon (m)

washing-up liquid صابون غسيل الصحون Saboon ghaseel iSSoHoon (m)

wastepaper basket سبت الزبالة sabat izzibaela (m)

watch ساعة sa'a (f)

to watch: he/she watches يتفرج/بتتفرج biyetfarag/bitetfarag

watch out! خد بالك khod baelak

water مياه maiya (f)

waterfall شلال shalael (m)

waterproof ووتر بروف watar broof

water-skiing التزحلق على الماء ittazaHloq 'ala il mae' (m)

wave موجة mowga (f)

way (path) طريق Taree' (m)

» that way من هناك min hinaek

» this way من هنا min hena

way in دخول dokhool

way out خروج khoroog

wax شمع sham' (m)

we احنا eHna

weak ضعيف/ضعيفة Da'eef/Da'eefa

weather الجو iggaw (m)

weather forecast النشرة الجوية innashra iggawaya (f)

web (internet) الوب il web

web designer مصمم/مصممة الوب سايت moSammim (m)/moSammimit (f) il websait

wedding فرح faraH (m)

week أسبوع izboo' (m)

weekend ويكند weekend (m)

weekly أسبوعي/أسبوعية isboo'i/isboo'aya

to weigh: he/she weighs يوزن/توزن yewzin/tewzin

weight وزن wazn (m)

well كويس/كويسة **kwaiyis/kwaiyissa**

well done برافو **braavo**

Welsh من ويلز **min waylz**

west غرب **gharb** (m)

western غربي/غربية **gharbi/gharbaya**

wet مبلول/مبلولة **mablool/mabloola**

wetsuit بدلة غطس **badlit ghaTs** (f)

what اية **ay**

wheat قمح **amH** (m)

to watch: he/she watches

wheel عجلة **'agala** (f)

wheelchair كرسي المتحوقين **korsi li mo'awaqeen** (m)

when امتى **emta**

where فين **fayn**

which (one) انهي/اي واحد/واحدة **waHid/waHda**

whisky ويسكي **wiski** (m)

white ابيض/بيضا **abyaD/bayDa**

white coffee قهوة بالبن **ahwa bil laban** (f)

who مين **meen**

whole كامل/كاملة **kaemil/kamila**

why لية **layh**

wide عريض/عريضة **areeD/areeDa**

widow ارملة **armala** (f)

widower ارمل **armal** (m)

wife زوجة **zowga** (f)

wild متوحش/متوحشة **motawaHish/motawaHsha**

to win: he/she wins يكسب/تكسب **yeksab/teksab**

» who won? مين كسب **meen kesb**

wind ريح **reeH** (m)

windmill طاحونة هوا **TaHoonit hawa** (f)

window شباك **shibbaek** (m) (shop) فترينة **vatreena** (f)

windscreen الزجاج الامامي **izzogaeg il amaemi**

windsurfing التزحلق الشراعي **tazaHloq shira'i** (m)

windy ريح قوية **reeH 'awaya** (f)

wine نبيذ **nebeet** (m)

wing جناح **ginaH** (m)

winter شتاء **sheta** (m)

with مع **ma'**

without من غير **minighayr**

woman امرأة **imra'a** (f)

wonderful مدهش/مدهشة **modhesh/modhesha**

wood خشب **khashab** (m)

wool صوف **Soof** (m)

work عمل **'amal** (m)

to work: he/she works يعمل/تعمل **ye'mil/te'mil**

» it works (functions) بيشتغل/بتشتغل **biyishtaghal/bitishtaghal**

world العالم **'alam** (m)

worried قلقان/قلقانة **al'aen/al'aena**

worse اسوا **aswa**

worth: it's not worth it ما يستهلش/تستهلش **ma yestahelsh/testahelsh**

would like احب **aHeb**

wound جرح **garH** (m)

to wrap: he/she wraps (up) يلف/تلف **yelif/telif** يدفي/تدفي **yedfi/tedfi**

wrist معصم **me'Sam** (m)

to write: he/she writes يكتب/تكتب **yektib/tektib**

writer كاتب/كاتبة **kaetib** (m)/ **kaetiba** (f)

writing paper ورق للكتابة **wara' lil kitaeba** (m)

wrong غلط **ghalaT** (m)

X

x-ray اشعة **ashe'a** (f) ghaseed

Y

yacht يخت **yakht** (m)

to yawn: he/she yawns يتثاوب/تتثاوب **yettaewib/tettaewib**

year سنة *sana* (f)
yellow اصفر/صفراء *aSfar/Safra*
yes ايوة *aywa*
yesterday امبارح *imbariH*
yet لسة *lessa*
yoghurt زبادى *zebaedi* (m)
you انت *inta* (to m)/*inti* (to f)/
انتم *entom* (to group)
young صغير/صغيرة *Soghaiyar/
Soghaiyara*
youth شباب *shabaeb* (m)
youth hostel بيت الشباب *bayt il
shabaeb* (m)

Z

zip سوستة *sosta* (f)
zoo جنينة الحيوانات *ginaynit il
Haiyawanaet* (f)

Now you're talking!

BBC Active offers a wide range of innovative resources, from short courses and grammars, to more in-depth courses for beginners or intermediates. Designed by language-teaching experts, our courses make the best use of today's technology, with book and audio, audio-only and multi-media products on offer. Many of these courses are accompanied by free online activities and television series, which are regularly repeated on BBC TWO Learning Zone.

Independent, interactive study course
2 x PC CD-ROM; 144pp course book;
60-min audio CD; free online activities
and resources www.getinto.com.

Travel pack
160pp book;
1 x 75-minute
CD.

Short independent
study course
128pp book;
2 x 60-minute CDs/
cassettes.

BBC ACTIVE

For further information on our language courses, or to buy online, visit www.bbcactive.com/languages. BBC Active titles are also available from bookshops, or by calling 0870 830 8000.